UNSTOPPABLE

THE YOUNG ATHLETE'S GUIDE TO ROCK SOLID MENTAL STRENGTH

THOMAS BOURNE

CONTENTS

INTRODUCTION

There are very few things as dramatic and captivating as competitive sports. Nothing compares to the adrenaline rush that comes with making a winning play just in the nick of time or scoring a new personal best in a race. Your heart is thumping in your chest, blood is coursing through your veins, and your muscles feel stronger than ever before. Every breath you take is focused and time seems to stop. The only thing that matters is the moment at hand when you know exactly what you need to do. You calculate each movement, every step, and remember the wise words from your coaches. As the clock hits zero, you make the perfect play that has won your team the game. Cheers erupt from the audience and pull you back to reality. People tell you that you are going places. You've done it.

Turning to your teammates, you notice the grins on each of their faces and the sparkle in their eyes. They're incredibly proud; you've all won together.

What makes the victory so sweet is that you made it happen. It was your team that put in countless hours of training and conditioning to get where you needed to be. You know exactly how many hours, drills, and practices it took to get to a level where you could even compete in the first place. There were days when you woke up early or stayed up late practicing, but it was all worth it. Your sport is what you love and winning was your dream. Your hard work is what made it a reality.

Even after incredible victories, so many athletes face a whole other set of challenges away from their games. With such pressure to perform at high levels, competitive sports are often the root of many mental health issues that can make it difficult to leave everything on the field. Whenever they set out to compete, athletes strive not only to meet their own expectations but also to live up to the expectations of their fans, coaches, families, friends, and teammates. They are encouraged to always be better than they were before, to set new personal bests, and to put everything they have into their work. In professional sports, fans glamorize athletes that train to the point of exhaustion and praise them for their work ethic. While some pressure can be good and encourage people to improve, constant stress can be extremely harmful.

Young athletes bear the burden of all of these expectations more than most. At a time when they are trying to figure out who they are and how to navigate the world, they are constantly being told to work, train, and deliver. They are expected to balance the demands of their sport with school, friends, family commitments, and part-time jobs. Still, their athletic pursuits continuously require more of their time and effort, which can leave them feeling burnt out and exhausted. Young people also process an incredible amount of media every day, which often depicts sports and ideas about how they should be training. They also compare themselves to their peers or professional athletes they see on television and social media and wonder whether they are good enough to keep performing. It doesn't take long for these feelings of inadequacy and anxiety to take over, impair performance, and cause people to shut down completely.

But they can't shut down. They love their sports and put all of their hearts and souls into training. To stop would be to give up on their dreams and on the dreams of everyone who has loved and supported them for their entire careers. To admit that they're struggling would feel like betraying their sports, which have brought them so many opportunities and so much joy over the course of their lives. What they want is to return to their sport the way it was when they first began, back when it was fun, exciting, and challenging. Back when it made them smile.

What makes these feelings so difficult to deal with is the fact that they are invisible. Coaches and fans can see what an athlete does, but not how they think and feel. It can be incredibly difficult to open up and talk about mental health, or even to find the right words to describe these issues in the first place! Often, problems are brushed aside with the mindset that "it's just a bad day" or "everyone gets nervous before a competition." While these things may be true, dismissing unpleasant feelings does not acknowledge why they might be there in the first place or how to cope with them in the future. Plus, they have a significant impact on an athlete's happiness and ability to keep doing what they love.

Fortunately, there are ways to manage these feelings and navigate the world of sports in a way that keeps athletes feeling capable, confident, and ready to perform. In this book, I discuss what it means to have mental toughness and outline strategies for setting goals, coping with disappointment, and finding a healthy mental headspace for competitive athletes. By implementing these strategies, young people should be able to take back control of their lives and focus on enjoying the sports they have worked so hard to train for.

I have long been fascinated by the human mind and how the way we think can help us achieve our goals. Sports have always been a passion of mine and something that I have found to be very achievement-oriented. In my experience, mindset plays a critical role in how I perform and how I feel about what I do. Playing tennis and rugby are things I always looked forward to, no matter what the outcomes of the matches might be. Not every game or every weekend goes exactly as planned, there are disappointments and difficult moments, but the mindset I have developed helps me see these as only temporary and a necessary part of the process that helps me achieve my end goals. The love I have for my favorite sports is what motivates me to return, and my mental toughness is what helps me persevere through challenging times.

The first step in developing mental toughness in the world of sport is understanding the invisible challenges that athletes endure every single day while they are planning, preparing, and training to compete. We must first consider what mental health means and how it is impacted by the demands of competing, which is something I will outline in the very first chapter. I hope you enjoy this book and that you find these strategies as helpful as I have when it comes to maintaining your mental health and playing your sport for the love of the game.

1

MENTAL HEALTH AND THE YOUNG ATHLETE

There's no question that being a competitive athlete is difficult. This is one of the reasons why we look up to Olympians and world record holders. Athletes push their bodies and minds far beyond what most people could even imagine. We often praise them for their discipline and willingness to make sacrifices in exchange for success. Most people, however, don't see what happens behind the scenes after the competition is over. An athlete's lifestyle is not always exciting or glamorous. Young athletes in particular often face unique challenges that go unrecognized.

For most young people, playing sports is just one part of their busy lives. They are so much more than just athletes. They are students, employees, family members, and friends, every part of their lives requires time and attention. It's essential that they dedicate time to their schoolwork to further their education and prepare themselves for their academic and professional goals in the future. Plus, for many people, there are certain grade requirements they need to meet in order to qualify for university programs or employment later on. Young athletes must figure out how to set aside study time between training sessions or complete assignments without having them interfere with competition days. This comes with its own stress, especially in their later years of study, when classes become increasingly more complex and require more of a student's attention.

In order to succeed in school, students also need to ensure that they get adequate sleep and nutrition. Teachers and professors often give the advice to not stay up all night studying before an important exam, knowing that their students will perform better having had a full night of sleep rather than a couple of extra hours reading. At a certain point, the human brain becomes so exhausted it cannot function properly and will not be able to solve problems. Good meals are also important, but it takes time to shop for, plan, and prepare nutritious meals. This can be difficult to do for someone whose evenings are occupied by long practices.

A lot of young people are also faced with financial challenges. Some may receive support from their family, which can go a long way towards helping them play their sports; but, for many, this is not an option. Young people may be expected to cover some or all of the expenses associated with their athletic pursuits, including paying for equipment, coaching, competition fees, travel, and uniforms. At very high levels of competitive sports, these fees can add up very quickly. This might mean athletes have to find ways to save money by opting out of competitions or training sessions or working more to get the funds they need. Working a part-time job can be a great way to build a resume and gain valuable workplace skills, but they can also be demanding and take up more time in an athlete's already busy schedule.

Family is another essential part of a young person's life. Whether their family is made up of blood relatives or people they have chosen to spend their time with, an athlete often finds that these people are their biggest fans and supporters. They are often the ones that drive the athlete to early morning practices, fuel them with home-cooked meals, and lend a listening ear after a frustrating game. It's important to keep relationships with family strong because these are the people athletes will rely on long after they are finished with their sports. Everyone wants to make time to spend with the people they love the most, and they don't want to feel like they are missing out when important events happen without them.

As amazing as families can be as a source of support, they can also present some other challenges for young people. Often, young people are expected to help with tasks or chores that benefit the family as a whole. They may need to act as caregivers for young children or older adults. This can be a lot to balance alongside school, a job, and the demands of training, competing, and performing.

With so much happening all at once, it is understandable that young people have stress coming from many different areas of their lives, and as a result, they may have less of a capacity to cope with stress related to competitive sports. It might also mean they have less time to dedicate to their chosen discipline than they would like, which can be stressful in and of itself, especially if they have coaches or teammates encouraging them to practice more. Time is a limited resource and for many young people, only a fraction of what they have can go towards their sport.

For a lot of athletes, there are people in their lives who are also invested in their performance. These people may include coaches, friends, partners, teammates, and for younger people, parents and teachers. Each of these people plays a role in helping someone play and excel in the sport they love, but having such a big support system can add to an individual's stress when performing. Sports people often feel that if they don't win or don't meet certain standards, they are disappointing the people who love them and who care about their success. They fear "letting them down" and put extra pressure on themselves with the goal of making others proud.

Young people also face unique challenges when it comes to social media. The current generation is able to communicate with each other and access information more quickly than ever before. For someone interested in sports, it's very easy to open a news article about professional athletes while waiting for the bus or scroll through Instagram posts from teammates about their most recent victories while relaxing before bed. In these cases, it's common for young people to compare themselves and their own lives to what they see online, which can change the way they think about their own performance.

The reality is that most of what we see on social media is the highlight reel of other people's lives. When someone makes a post, they often only share what is most significant or exciting to them. For athletes, these things might be competitions they have won, records they have set, or distinctions they have earned. What we don't see are the difficulties people face or the criticism they get, which can lead us to believe these things aren't there at all. When we compare ourselves to social media posts that are made, we can often feel inadequate because our difficult moments are not as exciting as someone else's victories. This is not a fair comparison to make. Just because someone does not directly post about their difficult moments does not mean they don't happen, and it certainly does not mean our victories aren't just as exciting as theirs.

HOW IT FEELS

When the pressures of performing and making time for competitive sports impact a young person's mental health, it affects the way they think about their sport. Many people started their participating in sports because their sport is something they love. It challenged them, excited them, and gave them something to work towards. They could feel themselves improving, but even when they were clumsy and made mistakes, they enjoyed going to practice. However, as athletes advance to a more competitive level, they often become less tolerant of their own mistakes and have an overwhelming desire to be perfect all the time. This is not realistic.

Every human being makes mistakes and has bad days. Instead of brushing these aside, it can be easy for athletes to become afraid of them. They become afraid to play the sports that once brought them joy for fear they will do something wrong. Their lives are spent wondering about how their next practice will go, and they cannot think about what has already gone well for them. They worry about being late for practices or missing important things, anxious over making a mistake with their schedules that will let down their coaches and teammates. Their sport becomes a burden rather than a positive addition to their lives.

If this happens, committing to a training and competition schedule can be incredibly exhausting. It takes a lot of physical and mental effort to attend practices, team events, and games. When events bring anxiety, people often dread them and are incredibly unhappy as they move from one commitment to another. They feel overwhelmed, and try to get out of things like social events where they can.

It is not surprising that feeling this way can impact an athlete's performance. By constantly thinking about what could go wrong, an athlete is less able to focus on the tasks at hand. They might have a knot in their stomach and be less able to concentrate in practice while their mind wanders. Their hands might shake, causing them to make mistakes they otherwise would not have made. They might be less able to socialize and connect with other members of their team, disrupting their relationships with the other people they spend their time with. All of these things might contribute further to the negative feelings they carry with them, creating a never-ending cycle of worry.

MENTAL HEALTH IN SPORT

Athletes spend a lot of time thinking about their health in order to maximize their performance. They think about the food they put into their bodies, their training schedules, and their doctor's appointments. They plan warm-up and cool-down routines to prevent themselves from getting injured. When an athlete is physically injured, it is commonly accepted that they will get help. They find medical professionals to care for them, use ice or bandages to help them feel better, or take rest days when they need them. They know that playing through an injury can often cause damage to their bodies that they can't repair. Getting help is critical for making sure they recover and can continue playing in the future.

The same cannot be said about mental health. We know less about it and unlike physical injuries, we can't always tell when someone is struggling with mental health unless they say something directly. This puts the burden on the person experiencing the issues to advocate for themselves, explain their difficulties, and ask for help, which is never easy. There is also an incredible amount of stigma around mental health conditions and how people are expected to manage them, which makes them even more difficult to talk about.

Mental health conditions are often thought of as "less than" physical injuries. Someone with a broken bone is allowed rest and take time to recover, while someone experiencing anxiety may have their concerns diminished and simply be told to "calm down." People who don't understand mental health issues may not realize that how a person feels and reacts in a given situation is not in their control, and advice like "calm down" is entirely unhelpful.

In sports, the pressure to "just work through" difficulties is even greater. Competitive athletes are used to being pushed to their limits. After all, challenging workouts are what allow people to grow. Exhaustion and sore muscles are facts of life for those training for competition. Often, when people need to take a break because of how they are feeling—physically or mentally—they are worried this is a sign of weakness. They don't want their coaches and teammates to think they aren't strong enough, and they want to prove to themselves that they can keep training. Time taken as a break is often seen as "lost time" that could otherwise be spent working towards their goals. This is where people will attempt to "push through" painful physical injuries and cause even more damage to their bodies. In these situations, the best thing an athlete can do is take a break and recover.

When athletes reach a point of exhaustion where they need a break from the demands of their sport but are unable to get one, thoughts of self-harm may develop. This stems from the idea that if the person were to develop an injury or illness that prevented them from competing, they would have permission to stop their sport and finally have the rest they need. Thoughts of self-harm are incredibly dangerous and need to be treated seriously. People experiencing this issue should seek professional counseling and work with their team —especially family and coaches—to come up with a plan that will allow them to take care of themselves.

We also live with the societal expectation that we need to be achieving all the time in order to have self-worth, an expectation that is only intensified in the world of competitive and professional sports. Athletes strive to achieve personal bests and always be stronger than they were the last time they competed. The media is full of information about people breaking world records or winning competitions that take incredible skill. This drive is part of what pushes people to excel and achieve their goals, but it can also be a source of constant pressure. Often, athletes are expected to play their sport, not simply because they love it, but because they should want to compete or turn it into a career for themselves. While these pathways may make certain people happy, they are not for everyone and may ultimately cause some people to feel unhappy with their sport.

In these cases, athletes are faced with an impossible choice. They can continue to train and compete with a schedule that does not make them happy, or they could quit and leave behind the sport they love. If they choose to return, their mental health may decline; if they choose to walk away, they will be abandoning everything they worked for. It's not an easy decision for any athlete to make. The challenge is to work toward making changes that allow the athlete to return to their sport and enjoy playing.

One common misconception, however, is that in order to have good mental health, one needs to be happy all of the time. This is far from the truth. It's normal to have good days and bad days. When something bad happens, it's okay to be sad or to feel a loss. Someone in a healthy mental state can take these emotions, process them, and continue to live their lives. They have the tools to get themselves through challenging times without feeling like they're out of control or like they are shutting down. Ultimately, these feelings should pass and people should be able to find joy in the things they love once again.

When these feelings don't pass, or if they become all-consuming, they could be symptoms of more serious conditions, like anxiety or depression. Not only do these make it difficult to enjoy playing sports, but they can also make it challenging to function normally in daily life. Depression can manifest as feelings of worthlessness or lack of interest in activities that were once exciting, which means that a person experiencing depression may struggle to find the motivation to do things like prepare meals, socialize with friends, or do household chores. Anxiety can make even small tasks feel overwhelming or prompt panic attacks that make it impossible for people to reason their way through day-to-day challenges.

One in four people have a mental health condition, but these conditions still remain heavily stigmatized (Garrick, 2017). Many people are hesitant to seek professional help for fear they will be labeled with one of these conditions, even if they could benefit from additional support. Conversations about mental health are often awkward and uncomfortable, making it difficult for people to ask questions or seek help. Starting conversations is often the most intimidating part. People are often unsure of who they can turn to, whether they can trust someone to take their concerns seriously, and how they can access resources in their community. Mental health resources are frequently not widely available, and if they are, they're not well advertised, so people must go out of their way to find and use them. This is not an easy task for someone who is already overwhelmed and struggling.

What is Actually Happening in the Brain

In many cases, mental health conditions, including depression and anxiety, can be attributed to chemical imbalances inside our bodies. While these may not explain everything that is happening with the way we feel, research has shown links between levels of these chemicals and mood. Two of the biggest contributors in these cases are dopamine and serotonin.

Whenever we think, move, or feel something, our brain sends lightning-fast electrical messages along special cells called neurons. These neurons are arranged in a complex network and connect with one another like links in a chain. Electrical impulses travel down the length of a single neuron, but when it comes to passing the message to the next link in the chain, we rely on chemicals called neurotransmitters to help us bridge the gap between cells. As a result, the neurotransmitters in our bodies play an important role in determining which messages get passed along, which ultimately affects the thoughts we have and the things we feel.

Serotonin and dopamine are both neurotransmitters linked to positive feelings. Dopamine is a major contributor to rewarding feelings and when it is low, it has been linked to symptoms of depression, including feelings of hopelessness or lack of interest in things that one usually finds interesting. Serotonin helps us process anxious feelings, and when it is imbalanced, one often has trouble processing difficult emotions (Medical News Today, 2022). To increase levels of these neurotransmitters, one can eat a balanced diet, including foods that are rich in the amino acid tryptophan. These foods include spinach, eggs, and chicken. Medical professionals also recommend activities including exercise and meditation to help boost serotonin and dopamine naturally, as well as getting enough regular, good-quality sleep.

These hormones are also the reason why some professionals will recommend antidepressant medications to certain patients. Even after making lifestyle modifications to manage mental health conditions, some people may still require more help because the imbalances of dopamine and serotonin in their brains are out of their control. These individuals may benefit from medications that could help them manage their condition and improve the way they feel.

HOW TO APPROACH MENTAL HEALTH IN SPORT

The issue of mental health is incredibly complex, and whether it is considered in the context of competitive sports or in everyday life, it needs to be recognized. Just because conditions like burnout, anxiety, and depression cannot be seen by an outside observer does not mean they don't exist and that they don't have a real impact on a person's life. They need to be talked about, prevented where possible, and treated properly when they do happen.

Understanding mental health is an important first step in caring for yourself and ensuring that you are in the best possible state of mind. Everyone faces challenges or difficulties. They are not a sign of weakness or lack of motivation, but rather a normal part of a person's experience, and athletes are no different. You owe it to yourself to be gentle and not critical when your sport becomes overwhelming. Only you can really understand your own feelings and what is happening in your own brain, which means you need to monitor your emotions and be your own advocate. Check in with yourself often to assess how you're doing overall. Do not be afraid to admit when you need help and ask for the support you need.

One of the best things that can be done for promoting mental wellness is to talk about it openly. When young athletes recognize that they feel unwell, they should be able to turn to a parent, coach, friend, or professional that they trust to make a plan about how to keep themselves healthy. It can be a good practice for coaches or team captains to organize regular mental health check-ins with their players or team members to provide opportunities for people to discuss concerns they may have. If this isn't something your team does already, make a suggestion!

When having these conversations with coaches and teammates, it's important to keep in mind that everyone has a different background and different levels of comfort when talking about mental health issues. Be patient with teammates who may be struggling but are having a hard time discussing their issues. As a team, you can make a safe, comfortable environment for people to bring forward the things that are bothering them, but never force someone to make a disclosure they aren't yet ready for, even if you are trying to be supportive. People may need some time to recognize when they need help and figure out who to seek support from. It's okay to say something like: "I'm here if you would like to talk" or "There has been a lot going on lately, I hope you know you can come to me if you ever need anything." This opens the door for communication and lets your teammates know that you care, but it gives them the ability to decide whether or not they would like to continue the conversation.

When someone does make a disclosure, take it seriously. It takes a lot of courage to talk about mental health and if someone raises an issue, there is a good chance they have been thinking about it for quite some time. Everyone asks for support and shows support in different ways. It can be helpful to ask teammates if there is anything you can do to help them or what they would like to see change moving forward. Sometimes there may be specific changes that can help a person recover, but sometimes people just need a friend and a listening ear. Both are equally important! Either way, when someone does make a disclosure, let them know their feelings are valid and be sympathetic that they may need some extra help for a little while.

For serious concerns, it's best that an athlete involves health care professionals in their journeys to recovery. Family physicians can be great places to start when trying to find resources to connect with. Schools and hospitals may also have mental health professionals that are familiar with helping athletes. Involving health care providers does not always mean a person will require medications or intensive treatment, all it means is that more people are available to support a person who needs it. If you believe that you or someone you know is in immediate danger because of a mental health condition, call emergency services in your area right away. There are community resources available to help people with urgent concerns and ensure everyone's safety.

2

THE IMPACT OF STRESS ON THE BODY AND ON PERFORMANCE

The human body is a complex system made of many interconnected working parts. Our bones support our muscles, and our muscles move our bodies. Our nerves communicate with our muscles to turn our thoughts into actions, and our blood runs through our veins to feed our cells and give us the energy we need to function. Every part of us is linked to the others in a complex web of signals and movements. We're like a machine, as soon as one part of us stops working, we cannot carry out the same activities we're meant for. The same can be said for our brains and overall mental wellness.

Our body goes through a series of changes in times of stress. In many ways, these changes are actually designed to help us. When early humans were in danger, for example, if they had to face a fierce predator, they had to act quickly and might not have a lot of time to calculate their response. They could fight the animal that was threatening them, run away from it, or freeze entirely, hoping it didn't see them. In any case, their response had to be automatic and instinct would take over as their body's stress response started to work.

In the modern world, we face far fewer dangerous threats than our ancestors did, but our stress response will still activate under certain circumstances. If we have a big game or are running late for practice, we are not in any physical danger, but our bodies react as if we are. The same sequence of changes will take place to prepare us for a fight, even if there is not necessarily anything to fight against. In these cases, the physiological changes aren't very helpful at all.

Initially, when we think about or see a stressful situation, we activate an area of our brain called the hypothalamus, which prompts our body to release a variety of signals. Some of these are electrical nerve signals, passed along by what is known as our sympathetic nervous system, while others are chemical signals in the form of hormones. These messages travel until they reach our adrenal glands, two small regions right on top of our kidneys, which secrete a substance called cortisol.

Cortisol is a hormone that is responsible for causing the body's long-term reaction to stress. It helps our tissues release stored sugar into our bloodstream so that it can be used for energy, it changes the way our brain uses its energy sources, and it helps us increase the availability of factors and proteins that are required to repair tissues. The main purpose of these changes is to help make sugars available for our muscles to use when either running or fighting, and prepare us to recover if we do experience an injury. When the stressor that we've encountered disappears, the level of cortisol in our bodies should decrease back to normal resting levels, and we stop producing more. This allows our organs to return to their usual functions.

Unfortunately, cortisol also slows down certain functions in our body that do not contribute directly to this initial "fight-or-flight" reaction. For example, it slows down our digestive system and impairs our immune function, which means we are more at risk for illness and infection. This is supposed to redirect resources to the systems that are needed right away, but if the fight-or-flight reaction is constantly engaged over an extended period of time, our bodies suffer if they have to do without the normal function of the other systems. It can also alter a person's sleep-wake cycle, making it difficult to get regular, quality sleep and alter growth, which could be an issue for young athletes whose bodies are still developing. Chronically high levels of cortisol have also been linked to other health issues including anxiety, depression, difficulties concentrating, heart disease, and headaches, all of which could affect an athlete's life significantly.

The good news is that there are several different ways a person can naturally reduce the cortisol levels in their body. Most of these strategies involve making healthy habits part of your lifestyle and reducing stress wherever possible. By eliminating stressful situations that can trigger the body's fight-or-flight response system, people can prevent the cascade of stress responses from even starting in the first place. For some athletes, this might involve looking at their schedules to see if there are commitments they can eliminate to help them feel less busy and more in control. However, it is not always possible to eliminate every stressful commitment, and athletes have busy schedules to begin with. It is not realistic to expect a schedule that is completely stress-free, but it is possible to work with stress and manage its effects. It's important to keep in mind that, while reducing stress and focusing on a healthy lifestyle is a great place to start to feel better, if you are experiencing health difficulties that concern you, the best thing to do is consult with a physician.

Examining your own thinking and recognizing stressful thoughts can be a great place to start when looking to reduce cortisol levels. In many cases, it's not the situations we're in that cause us stress, but rather our perception of these circumstances. If we tell ourselves we're in danger, we will believe we are and our bodies will react accordingly. However, stressful thoughts are just thoughts like any other and if we come to recognize them as such, we can acknowledge them rather than having them take control of us.

This can be done through a practice called "mindfulness." Mindfulness involves being an objective observer of what is going on inside and outside of our bodies. It means paying attention to our thoughts, letting them come and go without judgment, and noticing how they make us feel. We are not meant to criticize our thoughts, but rather recognize and process what types of thoughts trigger our stress response. Through regular mindfulness practice, many people can notice patterns of thoughts that make them feel worried. Perhaps they are always concerned about making a certain type of mistake during a competition or arriving late to practice. When these thoughts then reappear, it makes it easier to accept them as just thoughts rather than something that we need to be worried about.

Mindfulness can be a difficult practice for people to adopt, especially if it is not something they have ever done before. It can be overwhelming to try and acknowledge every thought that comes into your mind, but starting small can be a helpful strategy. Some find that setting aside a couple of minutes every day for reflection can be a great way to get started with the practice. This can be time set aside specifically for this purpose, or it could be quiet moments in their usual routine, like when they are on the bus or waiting for a class to begin. For some people, simply noticing thoughts as they come is enough to process them, while others prefer to write them down or say them out loud. In all cases, mindfulness strategies should make individuals more aware of the types of thoughts they find most stressful and may help them better process these thoughts.

Taking time to breathe is also a way individuals can reduce their cortisol levels in their everyday lives. While the stress response is partially triggered by the sympathetic nervous system, deep breathing exercises activate its opposite, the parasympathetic nervous system. This is activated when we are relaxed so that we can rest, recover, and carry out all of the regular processes our body needs to function, like digesting the food we eat. Some people like to use structured breathing techniques, like those practiced in martial arts or yoga classes, while others prefer to simply take long, deep breaths when they are feeling anxious. Both strategies have very similar benefits.

It can also be helpful for athletes to consider professional counseling to learn strategies that help them manage stress. Counselors are trained health care professionals who understand the stress response and are aware of tools and resources people might find helpful in their everyday lives. Some athletes like regular appointments with these professionals to talk about the things that are bothering them, while others find they only need a few appointments to learn strategies that work for them. Mental health counseling can be helpful for anyone who wants to learn about healthy ways to manage stress; it is not just for people with diagnosed mental health conditions. Some counselors even specialize in working with athletes and can discuss ways to manage specific issues like performance anxiety or sport-life balance. If you are interested in learning more about the professionals that might be available in your community, talk to your coach or reach out to local mental health organizations for more information.

One of the most important lifestyle modifications that an athlete can make to reduce stress and cortisol levels in their body is to ensure they are getting adequate sleep. It is currently recommended that all young adults aim to have eight hours of rest every night, although each person is different and some individuals may have slightly different needs. Athletes should set aside time every day to get the rest they need and set themselves up for quality sleep by making sure they limit light and noise in their bedroom if possible. Limiting interruptions by turning off phones and other electronic devices can also be a helpful strategy. Many people also find their sleep is better if they are on a reliable schedule. This means going to bed and waking up at the same time every day, including days off and weekends. It can be tempting to sleep in from time to time, but this often disrupts the body's rhythm. If athletes consistently get adequate sleep every night, they should still be rested even when waking up at a regular time.

The human body can come to expect time for sleep when it has a regular routine. The more an athlete commits to their bedtime schedule, the easier it will become for them to fall asleep at predictable times. A regular nighttime routine can also work very well. By taking some time to wind down with some relaxed activities at night, athletes can prepare their bodies to get the rest they need. People can choose any activity they enjoy but should avoid exercise for a few hours before trying to sleep.

In order to get good quality rest, it can be helpful to consciously practice good sleep hygiene and avoid things that might disrupt the body's ability to slow down at a reasonable hour. Caffeine in particular can help keep someone awake and stays in the body for up to six hours. It's good practice to avoid having any caffeinated teas, coffees, sodas, or chocolate several hours before bedtime in order to prevent them from interfering with sleep. Blue light, like that from phone or television screens, can also trick the brain into staying awake for extended periods of time. By limiting the use of electronics to approximately one hour before bed, some individuals may find it easier to fall asleep. Instead of using their devices, they can make it a regular practice to read, write, draw, or listen to music as part of their nighttime routine. If this is not possible, many electronics also have a setting that can be turned on to help block blue light, which may be an excellent alternative for when using a device directly before bedtime is necessary.

Exercise is another factor that can influence cortisol levels in the body, and it is one that athletes are very likely to be familiar with. It can have a variety of positive health effects including producing endorphins, which are natural feel-good chemicals that can boost mood, and improve sleep. Taking part in fun, moderate-intensity activities between training sessions, such as walking or bike riding, can be a great way to relieve stress, but it's important that athletes keep their own physical needs in mind. Too much activity has actually been shown to increase cortisol levels, which means taking breaks and rest days are incredibly important. When it comes to cortisol, too much activity is just as bad as too little.

The body is also able to produce endorphins, feel-good chemicals which help reduce stress, through laughing and smiling. Athletes can reduce cortisol in their own bodies simply by doing things that make them happy! This might mean spending time with friends, watching a funny movie, or taking in a comedy show. Some studies have also shown that taking part in other fun activities, like engaging in hobbies, can help reduce cortisol. Athletes might be able to reduce stress by learning a new language, playing an instrument, or doing any other activity they enjoy. In any case, taking time to unwind and laugh will feel good and help keep stress hormones within healthy limits.

The relationships a person has with other people in their lives can also play a significant role in their ability to manage stress in a healthy way. Friends and family can be excellent sources of support when athletes need advice or a listening ear. It can also be extremely comforting for someone to know there are people in their lives who unconditionally love and care for them. Research has shown that children who grow up in warm, nurturing family environments have lower levels of stress hormones in their bodies than those who face conflict. In addition, interacting with a loved one before a stressful event leads to a lower stress response overall. Even positive relationships with pets can be linked to lower levels of cortisol. It's important for athletes to take the time to foster positive relationships with the people who make up their support system in order to help them succeed in their sport.

It is important, however, that the people an athlete surrounds themselves with are supportive of their goals and athletic pursuits. Some friends or family members simply do not understand what an athlete's schedule is like and the types of difficulties they face. These people may try to diminish an athlete's concerns because their sport is "just a game" or because they think their own problems are more worthy of attention. These people can be toxic. They leave an athlete feeling frustrated and invalidated rather than supported. In cases like these, young people might choose to spend less time with the people who take their success away from them and more time with the ones that offer them the help they need. These might not always be people the athlete is directly related to; instead, they may be close friends or teammates. People like this will become like an athlete's chosen family and will still be an important support network for them.

Athletes know that the food they use to fuel their bodies can have a significant impact on the way they feel and perform. This is also the case when it comes to mental health and managing stress. Some researchers have shown that people who regularly consume a diet high in added sugar are more likely to have higher levels of cortisol than those who do not, suggesting that by limiting their sugar intake, athletes may be able to reduce the amount of cortisol in their bodies. This might involve reducing their consumption of sugary snacks, like cookies and cakes, as well as other processed foods which might contain artificial sweeteners. Snacks like granola bars often have ingredients like corn syrup added to them, which means people eating the food are consuming high amounts of sugar even though they think they're making a healthy choice. In many cases, it's possible to find recipes for these kinds of foods and make them at home, which gives consumers more control over their sugar content.

Reading product labels and choosing low-sugar options can also be an excellent strategy to use when shopping.

Soft drinks and sports drinks are other major sources of sugar to consider when examining one's diet. Drinks like sweet teas or sodas often have impressive amounts of sweeteners added to each serving. Substituting water or milk for soft drinks is a small change that can help athletes drastically reduce their sugar intake. It can still be possible to enjoy these types of beverages occasionally as a treat, but athletes should be mindful of how often and how much they are consuming.

While some foods should be cut out, certain foods have also been linked to lower levels of cortisol. Green tea contains a substance called L-theanine, which has been associated with lower levels of this stress hormone. Healthy fats, like those in nuts and avocado, can be excellent for brain function and mental well-being. Dark chocolate contains substances called flavonoids, which can help reduce cortisol levels by slowing its release from the adrenal glands in the first place. Finally, fresh fruits and vegetables contain important vitamins and minerals the human body needs as well as substances called antioxidants that help protect cells, including those in the brain, from damage, which promotes overall well-being.

Consuming probiotics can also be helpful for promoting mental health and lowering levels of stress hormones. In the human digestive system, there are millions of good bacteria that help us by promoting the breakdown of food and preventing the growth of harmful bacteria that could make us sick. Probiotics are bacteria that can help people maintain the colonies they have in their guts. They can be found naturally in foods like yogurt and sauerkraut, but they can also be purchased as tablets or capsules from health food stores. Research has found links between healthy gut bacteria and improved mental well-being, which suggests that making a conscious effort to help these bacteria thrive may reduce overall stress levels.

In addition to paying attention to the foods they eat, athletes should also be mindful of what they drink and whether they are consuming enough fluids over the course of their days. Dehydration can be associated with increased cortisol levels and can lead to an athlete suffering from physical and mental symptoms. It's important to remember to drink plenty of fluids before, during, and after training sessions, especially in warm weather. Athletes lose a lot of water through sweat and heavy breathing, which needs to be replaced in order to function normally. They should ensure they have access to water while playing their sports and that they continue to drink even once they are finished being active for the day.

Athletes may also need to take additional supplements alongside healthy diets to promote mental well-being and reduce their levels of stress hormones. For example, fish oil contains healthy omega-3 fatty acids, which are linked to lower levels of cortisol. It can be purchased as capsules at drug stores and grocery stores. Another herb called ashwagandha has been shown to reduce anxiety in randomized controlled trials and has been used in traditional medicine for years. If an athlete is interested in experimenting with natural supplements, it is a good idea for them to talk to a doctor or health care professional beforehand. These people are experts in their fields and understand what substances may or may not be a good fit for a specific patient. It is also important to ensure that all herbs and oils come from reputable sources and that the individual is not taking more than the amounts recommended by the manufacturers and health care providers.

The human body has an automatic reaction to stress, which can be helpful in the short term, but after an extended period of time, it can impact an athlete's ability to perform and have negative health impacts. By making a conscious effort to manage stress in their lives, athletes may be able to reduce the amount of stress hormones they have in their bodies. An individual can also promote mental well-being by making sure they get enough sleep and proper nutrition. Only by looking after themselves and making their health a priority will athletes be able to feel and perform at their very best.

3

EVEN THE BEST FALL SOMETIMES

It's no secret that every young athlete looks up to the "greats" in their sport. There are certain people who have managed to achieve greatness in their area of competition, setting world records or carrying out impossible feats, and will always be seen as examples of the "perfect" player. When these athletes are portrayed in the media, it's easy to view them as winners who have the best lives possible. They are playing the sport they love, have fans around the world cheering them on, and are incredibly successful while doing it. What is less talked about is the fact that many of these people have also experienced mental health difficulties that have interfered with their abilities to either play their sport or carry out their normal daily activities.

This chapter will share some stories about professional athletes who have spoken up about their own struggles with mental health and what they have done to help manage it. These people have demonstrated that having difficulties managing mental well-being is incredibly common, and, more importantly, that it is possible for athletes to have successful careers while still prioritizing their own physical and mental health. Injury and disappointment are common parts of an athlete's journey, and while they might not be easy to process, it is possible to work through them.

ATHLETE STORIES

Michael Phelps

Michael Phelps is a competitive American swimmer and the most decorated Olympian of all time, having taken home 28 medals from races he's won against some of the best athletes in his sport from across the world (O'Leary, 2022). He began his career by breaking his first world record at 15 years old, but Phelps has always pushed himself to train harder and improve, which has contributed significantly to his success. However, he has claimed that even after his incredible victories, he felt depressed after each set of Olympic Games. His depression then led to drug and alcohol abuse. Phelps claimed that his use of these substances was his attempt to escape the issues that were bothering him, but he later regretted some of the decisions he made (Scutti, 2018). In 2014, he was charged—for the second time in his life—for driving under the influence of alcohol after which he began to open up publicly about the problems he was dealing with (McDowell, 2021).

Michael Phelps revealed that there were times in his life when his mental health was so poor he was unable to eat, sleep, or carry out his normal activities for days at a time. He explained that during these periods he wanted to end his life and knew that he needed professional help. Phelps sought treatment at a rehabilitation center and began to speak more about the difficulties he endured. He feels that it is important to talk about mental health and that people need to know they can open up when they are struggling. Today, he advocates to help end the stigma around mental illness and is a spokesperson for an online therapy app. Phelps hopes that by sharing his own story, he can encourage others in a similar position to do the same and seek help when they need it.

It is not always easy to open up about mental difficulties in the way Phelps did, but for a lot of people, it can be a very positive experience. He claims that in his journey, he learned it is "okay not to be okay" and he credits a lot of the progress he has made to discussions with others about mental health (Scutti, 2018). While receiving treatment, Phelps was encouraged to talk about his feelings and admitted that once he began this practice, it became easier to process the things that were happening in his life. Young athletes should also trust that they can discuss their own feelings about playing their sports with their family members or coaches whenever they need to. When something comes to mind, talking through the issue can be a healthy way to process it and prevent feeling upset by it in the long term.

Naomi Osaka

Naomi Osaka, the number two singles tennis player in the world, made the difficult decision in 2021 to withdraw from the French Open tournament for mental health reasons (McDowell, 2021). Her decision to not participate would have been a complicated choice for any athlete to make. She trained incredibly hard for this competition and had fans who were looking forward to seeing her at the event. In this case, Osaka prioritized her own well-being over the tournament, and she received an incredible amount of support from other athletes who play the sport, including Serena Williams. Osaka explained how she had been struggling with depression since 2018, and leading up to the French

Open, she experienced a lot of anxiety regarding speaking at press conferences. As a professional athlete, she felt a lot of pressure when it came to speaking at these events and giving the best answers she possibly could to interviewers and the people who watched her compete. This became overwhelming to deal with.

Because she made the decision she did, Osaka was able to give herself more time and space to recover and prioritize her mental wellness, which will set her up for success in future competitions. Athletes often experience pressure to "push through" difficulties where they can, especially in competitions, and are worried that taking breaks will be seen as a sign of weakness or "giving up." Osaka's story shows that it is possible for athletes to care for themselves when it matters most. If she had competed at the French Open while she was struggling with her mental health, she would not have performed well and may have caused herself even more anxiety. It takes courage to step down from commitments in the way she did, but sometimes it is a necessary decision. Athletes need to have the confidence and strength to advocate for themselves as Osaka did.

Coaches and family members can also be an incredible source of support for young people. They can remind athletes that they can still be successful in their sport even if they don't compete in every race or game. If people are feeling overwhelmed, they need to be made aware that taking time off is an option for them, just like Osaka did, and they can work with their support team to make a plan about how they can return once they are feeling better. Ultimately, athletes need their support systems to advocate for them when they need to make a difficult decision like this one. They must all have the person's best interest in mind and keep their mental and physical well-being a priority.

Aly Raisman

After winning six Olympic medals in gymnastics, Aly Raisman retired from her sport in 2020, but she continues to make managing her mental wellness a priority. She now speaks about how she is recovering from past trauma and how every day is different when it comes to her mental health. Some days are more difficult than others, and she has said that it is difficult to predict how she will feel on any given day. Raisman highlights how managing her mental health is a process and not something that can be fixed completely overnight. She has had years of reflection and therapy to get herself to the point she is currently at, and she plans to keep working to find things that will help her in the future. Her commitment to managing her own wellness is inspiring, and it is true that recovery is a nonlinear process. Just because people can have some days that are more difficult than others does not mean that they are not making progress where it matters. Raisman continues to advocate for mental health and healing, especially for those who have experienced traumatic events in their past.

DeMar DeRosan

Basketball star DeMar DeRosan recently opened up to a newspaper in Toronto, Canada about mental health in professional athletes and his own struggle with depression. He wants the public to know that even though professional athletes are portrayed as "indestructible" and appear to have everything they could possibly need, they are still human and feel overwhelmed from time to time (Smith, 2018). Feelings of loneliness and disappointment are still normal, even for people who have an entire team and fan community supporting them. It might not be obvious to an outside observer that someone is having difficulties, but that does not mean they are not still working through challenges.

DeRosan opened up about his difficulties with a comment about depression on his Twitter account in 2018 and was met with incredible support from his fans. His post was an act of subtle advocacy. He opened up to the world about what he was experiencing in his own way, showing that these types of feelings are real and that it is okay to talk about them. In an interview, he claimed that his intent was simply to show that as an athlete, he also "goes through it" but is still able to be successful in his field (Smith, 2018). When people like DeRosan speak up, it can inspire others to do the same.

Tyson Fury

Tyson Fury is a British athlete with a 14-year-long career as a professional heavyweight fighter who has competed across the world and won some of the biggest fights in professional boxing. Like many athletes in many sports, it was not an easy task for Fury to reach world-class status. Fury struggled with motivation, weight gain and drug abuse, and this affected his mental well-being. In 2011, Fury spoke in an interview with *The Guardian* about feeling depressed and having thoughts of ending his life. Even a year after defeating Wladimir Klitschko, the reigning heavyweight world champion, in 2015 these thoughts and feelings persisted. Fury stopped competing for two and a half years. He spoke about how his depression led him to stop training, have increasingly dangerous thoughts, and begin using cocaine. This meant he did not pass drug testing and was "medically unfit" to compete in his sport. Because of this, he lost titles he had earned to other athletes who were allowed to compete (Farell, 2022).

Despite battling mental illness and not competing for several years, Tyson Fury returned to the heavyweight world in 2018 after a struggle to regain his boxing license. He fought against Deontay Wilder three times between 2018 and 2021. These fights were epic, arguably some of the most impressive and entertaining heavyweight fights of all time. Fury then fought what he claimed would be his last battle against Dillan Whyte in April 2022 in front of a crowd of 94,000 people at Wembley Stadium (Farell, 2022). Tyson Fury is an excellent example of someone who worked incredibly hard to overcome significant obstacles in both life and in the ring, which helped him achieve the goals he set out for himself when he first began his career. His journey and the challenges he has overcome are truly inspirational. He speaks openly about the mental health issues he has faced and how he has picked himself up numerous times. Any young athlete needing some inspiration or a real life story of going from hero to zero back to hero should look him up.

Young athletes aren't the only ones that experience mental health difficulties when training for and competing in their sports. Many professional athletes have also come forward with their own stories, especially after they have sought help or advocated for their own well-being. It's important that young people understand that when they feel overwhelmed or depressed, they aren't alone and that even the people who are most successful in the world of sports have experienced similar difficulties in their lives. What matters is that these people were able to get the help they needed, work on themselves, and return to doing what they love, which has allowed them to be the great athletes the world knows they are.

4

THE UNLIMITED POWER OF YOUR SUBCONSCIOUS MIND

Our brains are fascinating. They hold a wealth of knowledge and information that helps guide us through the steps involved with walking, talking, breathing, and completing everyday tasks. We use them to remember the coaching we have received, know the rules of the games we play, and strategize as we work towards bringing home a victory. We are, however, only aware of a small fraction of what happens in our heads. A lot of the brain's work happens "behind the scenes" and is operated by our subconscious mind.

For something that we might not notice on a regular basis, our subconscious mind has an incredible ability to store and recall important information. For example, some drivers will claim that every once in a while they forget details from their commute home from work because they were driving on "autopilot." Their subconscious took over, and they were able to navigate the familiar route without paying too much conscious attention. Similarly, athletes often practice drills and maneuvers over and over again until they can perform them without thinking. Their subconscious brain does all of the work for them, allowing them to focus on other parts of their drill or strategy. In this way, athletes are very familiar with the power of the subconscious mind and frequently use it to their advantage.

Our subconscious also works with several different systems in our body to maintain control in a world full of chaos. It helps maintain what is known as homeostasis, or a steady state. This is critical in order for our bodies to be able to function. We are designed to operate at a certain temperature and a certain chemical makeup. Our heartbeats and breathing follow predictable rhythms that ensure our cells receive a constant supply of oxygen and nutrients. When we change the environment we're in, our body works hard to make adjustments that will allow our internal conditions to stay the same. We don't need to think about making any of these changes, like changes in our heart rate or breathing, they just happen. Our subconscious mind has learned exactly what to do and takes care of the problems for us.

We also have homeostasis when it comes to the way we think and act. Our subconscious mind keeps us behaving in a certain manner consistent with our personality and beliefs. It has a series of unwritten rules that it follows when helping us shape our speech, reactions, and mannerisms. These can be influenced by our emotions and past experiences. Like homeostasis in our physical bodies, we don't always have a lot of control over our subconscious mind's immediate actions. Instead, it just follows what it has been told by our conscious thoughts in the past. This can sometimes cause us problems, especially if our subconscious mind has adopted the habit of jumping right to negative reactions.

Our subconscious minds learn their instructions in a variety of different ways. Genetics sometimes play a significant role, which means that some people are more likely to respond negatively to a situation than others. The most influential factor in changing the way we react, however, is what we have experienced in the past. We might have been conditioned to respond a certain way to a situation, based on the way we saw our parents and caregivers behave while we were growing up. Our reactions may also be a response to a traumatic event. If we have had something terrible happen to us, our subconscious mind may try to protect us from getting hurt in the future by causing us to react and behave in a certain way. We may not be aware of what shaped our subconscious minds, and we may not feel it happening, but we are always learning and changing as we move through life.

Just because we don't have much control over our subconscious mind as it is working does not mean we cannot influence what it does. This part of our brain operates much like a computer program; it does not reason its way through problems, it only reacts in the way it was told to. It is given a piece of information and behaves just like it is programmed to. The program, however, is written by our conscious mind, and it has the ability to make changes that can impact the way our subconscious works moving forward. We can use this to our advantage. If we make the right effort, we can make positive changes that our subconscious will use whenever it makes decisions in the future. These can be instrumental in establishing mental toughness and making habits that allow for our well-being.

POSITIVE AFFIRMATIONS

Positive affirmations are one important tool athletes are able to use to change the way their subconscious mind works and program it into positive thinking. These are short, positive words or phrases we repeat to ourselves as we live our lives. The idea behind using these phrases is that by consciously thinking about them over and over, we can program them into our subconscious mind and change the way it works. Affirmations can help us overwrite the negative thoughts or reactions we may have adopted and build new habits around positive thinking. With enough repetition, the positive reactions these phrases reinforce can become automatic to us, leaving us feeling happier and more empowered every day.

Affirmations take positive thoughts and express them in language we can process and understand. Our minds learn well by hearing and reading words, which means that well-crafted affirmations can teach us well. The more we repeat something, the more our minds understand that it is important; affirmations work best when we use them over and over again. Research involving MRI scans has even shown that self-affirmation tasks can cause the human brain to make different connections and rewire itself (Life Coach Directory, 2020). By using these as tools, we can literally change the way our minds work without even noticing.

On a more conscious level, affirmations can be a constant reminder of our goals and values. If we return, every single day, to stating the principles that are most important to us, we are more likely to think about them when making decisions, which can lead us to make choices we genuinely think are fulfilling. The ideas we choose to repeat remain at the front of our minds rather than getting lost among the other thoughts we are processing at any given moment. They have the ability to keep us focused. By reminding ourselves of what our goals are and where we want to be, we are more likely to take the steps we need to get there.

How to Use Affirmations

Affirmations can be helpful in a variety of different areas in someone's life, including their professional careers, relationships, body image, and self-esteem. Depending on what an athlete is looking for help with, they may wish to choose sports-related affirmations or general affirmations about themselves or their lives. The goal is for the athlete to develop a phrase or thought that is meaningful to them. This must also be a phrase they personally believe in. If a phrase does not reflect a person's own goals or core values, their subconscious mind will not embrace it, and it will not be able to make the positive changes affirmations are designed to do.

For people who don't know where to begin, there are a variety of online affirmation websites or mobile apps that are available free of charge. These might not have phrases that are specific to a particular athlete, but they do have some examples of positive phrases people may be able to repeat to themselves. These phrases may spark ideas for other, more specific affirmations that can come later on. Some applications might suggest a new word or phrase every day, which might help athletes make a habit of thinking about these sentences.

For athletes who have used affirmations before or who are interested in designing their own meaningful phrases, it can often be helpful to take some time to reflect on what a helpful affirmation should say. Some people may find that it is easiest to start by brainstorming all of the qualities they feel makes them a good athlete or a good person. At this stage, asking friends and family members can also be an incredible source of help, since the people who spend the most time with us often come up with ideas that we might not think of ourselves! These qualities can sometimes become the best affirmations. Repeating things like "I am strong" or "I am kind" can remind people of the things that make them so incredible, which often get lost when they are stuck in negative thinking patterns.

It can then be helpful for an athlete to examine some of the negative thoughts they are having. These are often the things that cause the most anxiety and distress. This may take some time, but simply noticing and recording negative or intrusive thoughts can be important for determining what areas affirmations should target.

Athletes can then work on translating these thoughts from negative ideas to positive, constructive phrases that represent what they would like to be moving forward. For example, a thought that might come when taking a break, like "I am lazy," might be translated to "I deserve the time it takes to care for myself." Something like "I'm not fast enough" or "I make too many mistakes" might become "I get faster and faster every day" or "I always make the best decisions I can." Above all, athletes must translate these statements into phrases that feel comforting and are things that they enjoy hearing.

Affirmations should also use the first person. When we use them, we are speaking to ourselves about ourselves. "I" statements are often the most powerful things we can use. Instead of saying things like "all people are worthy," we can say "I believe all people are worthy,'" or to make it even more personal, "I am worthy." Statements like these help us see ourselves in our affirmations and make them feel more relevant to us, which means our minds pay closer attention. Keeping statements in the present tense will also make them easier to process. Starting phrases with "I am" or "I feel" can help us make simple, impactful phrases.

Repetition is another important factor in having affirmations work in the way they are intended to. Reprogramming the subconscious mind is an incredible undertaking, especially after it has spent years learning how to think a certain way. Affirmations use the conscious mind to impress ideas upon the subconscious mind; the way we achieve that is through repetition. Every time we see and hear something, our brains have the ability to learn from it, and we want to make sure we are creating as many opportunities for improvement as possible. Many life coaches will recommend that you say affirmations at least once a day. It can be helpful for people to make repeating affirmations part of their daily routine, to ensure that they don't forget about them. Saying phrases while doing things like getting dressed in the morning or driving to school could be great times for athletes to make a habit of using affirmations.

Some people also like to be creative with how they use these tools. While simply saying affirmations out loud can be very effective, some people prefer to listen to or read these meaningful phrases. Making notes or posters with affirmations can be great ways for athletes to incorporate this tool into their daily living space, especially if they post them around places they look at frequently, like around mirrors or in bedrooms. People may also wish to write affirmations in places like day planners or on the lock screens of their phones so that they can see them and carry them around throughout their days. Listening to recordings of affirmations can also be an excellent strategy. People may create these recordings themselves or find available ones on sites like YouTube. No matter what they choose to do, as long as athletes are engaging with their affirmations on a regular basis, they will have the desired effect.

It is important to remember that even with frequent repetitions, affirmations will take time to work. Athletes cannot expect to see immediate changes in the way they think or feel overnight. They must have faith that, if they're committed, they will make progress and that every repetition is helping. This is why it is incredibly important to choose phrases that are meaningful and can be repeated over long periods of time. Results will happen, especially when affirmations are used to help people grow and foster positive thinking in the long term.

THE POWER OF POSITIVE THINKING

There are many misconceptions that exist when it comes to what it actually means to "think positive." It's often used as a catchphrase that promises to completely turn someone's life around. No matter what might be happening in their world, if they choose positivity, it will change everything. In many ways, positive thinking is described to be as easy as flipping a switch, something everyone can "turn on" if they simply decide to do it. Many people consider "positive thinking" to mean ignoring thoughts that aren't constructive and brushing them away like they simply do not exist. In reality, this is far from true.

Positive thinking isn't focused on banishing negative thoughts, but rather on controlling them and creating an environment that makes it more difficult for them to appear in the first place. It involves maintaining a mindset that diminishes the power of these negative ideas and focuses on the positive. This is something that takes continuous commitment and reflection, but it can have an incredible impact on the way an individual views their world. Even making small modifications in the way they choose to think about the things that happen in their lives can go a long way towards helping athletes develop their subconscious minds and embrace positive thinking.

This type of mindset is focused around the expectation that good things will happen. It is always anticipating the best, not preparing for the worst. As human beings, we often pay more attention to the things we expect to see. We're looking more closely for them and when we do see them, they confirm what we already believe to be true about the world. When we're in a positive state of mind, we are more likely to see the good things that happen around us and attract more positivity in our own lives. Others are likely to notice the positivity we bring with us every day and will, more often than not, respond favorably. By having a positive mindset, we will see more positivity returning to us from others. This does not mean we will never have bad days, it means we are actively looking for the things that will serve us well and embrace them when they come.

Training the Subconscious Mind

We can, of course, choose to focus on these positive things when we do see them. In every experience we have, there will be moments that make us happy and moments we like less. It is almost certain that we will have a better experience if we decide to focus on those moments that make us smile. For example, after driving to a competition, an athlete could either choose to focus on the traffic jam that caused them delays or the time they spent with friends along the way. If their focus stays on the traffic, they will undoubtedly feel annoyed and upset that their trip took longer than planned, but if they focus on their friends, they can still acknowledge that they would have preferred a shorter trip but will look back on it with happier memories. In this case, the athlete was able to reframe their experience in a way that is more positive and that will bring them more happiness overall.

One of the best things an athlete can do to foster positive thinking is to start considering themselves in control of their world. Rather than seeing major life events as things that happen to them, athletes can reframe these accomplishments as things they manifested. They did not simply "get lucky" because they won a race or competition, they were the one who made the victory possible because they trained for it. When people start to think in this way, they begin to appreciate the power they have in the world and their ability to achieve what it is they value most. This is often referred to as an "internal locus of control." A person perceives that the ability to control what happens lies within them rather than with someone else.

Similarly, once people understand their ability to control their own fate, they also understand the power they have to get themselves out of difficult situations. People who have this internal locus of control know they can fix their problems instead of having to live with an uncomfortable situation. When they are faced with something unexpected, such as losing a competition or having a disagreement with a teammate, their mind automatically starts to think through ways of dealing with the issue. They do not simply accept that these things have happened and wait for them to pass, they actively work to get themselves where they need to be moving forward.

The way athletes present themselves can also have an impact on the way they think and feel. People express their thoughts in many ways, including the way they dress, their body language, and how they treat others around them. When they feel overwhelmed, it might impact the way they look. They might slouch or appear more disheveled than they normally would. However, this has the potential to work both ways. People who put in the effort to stand up straight often move through their days with more confidence. Others will notice and will usually respond positively as well. This can be a very easy strategy to adopt. When an athlete feels themself slouching, they can sit up straighter and remind themselves of all the amazing things they are accomplishing every single day.

In addition to paying attention to posture, some people like to take advantage of other, less conventional "power poses" to boost their confidence. Standing like a superhero with their hands on their hips or spreading their arms and legs out wide like a star can make them feel like they are ready to take on the world. This can be a fun strategy for athletes to try before a big game or even a class presentation, as it might help them feel ready to take on the challenge that lies ahead. The more confident a person is, the more relaxed they will be heading into a performance, which usually helps them be more successful.

In addition to the way they present themselves, an athlete's words also hold an incredible amount of power when it comes to shaping their mindset. Language has the ability to make people feel emotions, and certain words carry more emotion than others. When comparing the words "terrified" and "nervous," most people would agree that "terrified" implies a stronger reaction and may evoke stronger feelings than the word "nervous." The words a person uses when talking to themselves can also have an impact on how they perceive their situation. If they are consistently using negative, emotional terms when thinking about inconveniences that happen in their lives, it will be more difficult for them to embrace a positive mindset.

People may be able to improve their mindset by considering the language they use when describing important events. When they catch themselves using an emotionally-loaded term, they can stop and consider whether they actually meant to use a term that strong or whether there is a more positive alternative to describe the situation better. Did they "hate" the meal they had for dinner, or were they just "disappointed" it didn't quite turn out how they intended? Are they "angry" with their friends, or are they "annoyed" with something they did? It can often be helpful to keep a running list of some of these negative terms that come up frequently and record some other words that could be used in their place. This way, if people ever feel stuck when describing a situation, they can refer to their other options and choose one that works better.

It is also incredibly important that when people are looking to transform their mindsets, they are surrounding themselves with the right support system. Athletes need people who will help build them up, not those who are toxic and will take away from their success. They need to spend their time with people who are positive thinkers, not people who complain and are unhappy with their own lives. This unhappiness will make it difficult for someone who is putting forward the effort to break free from bad habits. Athletes get to choose who they surround themselves with and they deserve to connect with people that help them be the best they can be. If they start to notice a group has a tendency to always complain or frame situations in a negative light, it might be worth having a conversation with them about positive thinking, if the individual feels comfortable. If this does not work, they may want to consider spending some more time away from the group to focus on their own development.

Just like how lifting weights becomes easier with frequent training, positive thinking becomes embedded in the subconscious mind with effort and practice. Even if they don't notice major changes right away, athletes will still benefit from training their subconscious over time. Repetition and consistency are key. The more a person reframes their thoughts, puts themselves in control, and questions the language they are using, the more these positive corrections will become habit.

5

CRYSTAL CLEAR GOALS

Whether they're training on the field or completing a class project, athletes always seem to be working for a reason. They have an end result in mind and are putting forth the effort to get there. The athlete is on a journey and their goal is their final destination; however, the road map to that destination is not always clear. Sometimes people have a rough idea of where they would like to be, but they don't necessarily know how to get there. In each case, there are obstacles to overcome that make the end goal more difficult to reach. When these come up, it is even more important than ever for people to have something to work towards to keep them motivated.

Goal setting is an important skill for all young people to develop, both inside and outside the world of sport.

Not only does it give people something to work towards, but it can also help them stay focused enough to actually get there. If they know where they are going, they can plan their training and activities accordingly so that the things they are doing bring them closer to where they would like to be. It also means they can assess their own progress. Knowing how close they are to their goals allows athletes to determine how far they have come since starting and what else they need to do to reach their end result.

For athletes, it's often important to start the goal-setting process by reflecting on what it is they would like from their sport. Why did they start playing? What makes a competition or practice good for them? Some people compete simply because they enjoy it, or they do it for the team environment. Others want to turn their sport into a career or compete for scholarships at universities. Certain athletes find motivation in breaking records and achieving their own personal bests in their area of play and are always galvanized by their next victory. Everyone has a very different set of motivating factors that prompt them to keep working hard, but it can be difficult to figure out exactly what they are.

A useful daily practice before going to sleep each night is envisioning the end result you wish to manifest in your mind. During this practice, picture the goal being realized as something that is happening right now. Add emotion to the scene in your mind and allow yourself to feel it like you have just achieved the goal you have been working so hard toward. See the desired end result in your mind. Some questions that can direct this practice are: What does success mean to you? Picture a moment in the future when you have achieved your goals in your sport. Think about what is all around you and allow the moment to play like a video in your mind. What sounds do you hear? What does it smell like? When you look around, you notice there are people all around you. Who is there? They might be the people who have helped you on your journey or the most important people in your life How does this picture look? How does it make you feel? Some athletes know the answer to every single one of these questions, while others might be less sure. The video in their minds is cloudy and they can't quite see every detail. And that's okay! A person's goals and idea of success might shift over the course of their lives, and this is very normal. This chapter will outline strategies for setting crystal clear goals and giving athletes concrete objectives they can work towards in order to make their vision of success a reality.

SETTING GOALS

While there is no "right" or "wrong" way to set a meaningful goal, one strategy that many athletes find helpful is setting SMART goals. Each letter in this acronym stands for an aspect of the goal, which allows people to plan their objectives in detail. The more specific the goal, the better! Knowing more about where they would like to go means people will be sure when they have achieved success and have an easier time planning out how to get there.

S–Specific and Significant

The first step in setting a SMART goal is to come up with an idea for the goal itself. What is it that the athlete actually wants to accomplish? This aim might be related to their performance in their sport or in how they manage their everyday lives. The important part, however, is that this goal is specific. An athlete should know exactly what they want and how they will know once they have achieved it. For example, it's not enough to simply say "I will be faster in my races." While someone may, in fact, want to be faster, this goal does not tell them exactly how fast they would like to be. In this case, it might be a better practice to have a specific time they would like to beat in their race so that they have something concrete to aim for. The goal could also revolve around a specific event or tournament. For example, an athlete could set a goal of winning a tournament or scoring a certain number of points in a specific game.

The goal must also be significant. It is something the athlete will be dedicating their time towards, and it must be a big enough goal to actually be challenging. Growth and improvement only happen when people are pushed to try new things. If an athlete sets a goal that is beyond their current capabilities, but still realistic to achieve, they will work harder and feel a greater sense of pride when they actually reach it.

M-Measurable and Meaningful

A measurable goal challenges athletes to think about what they will use to assess their progress while they are working toward their goal. For some tasks, this may be easy. People can measure the amount of weight they lift, the amount of time it takes for them to run a certain distance, or the exact grade they earn on a test or assignment. For outcomes that are more difficult to measure, such as being kinder to others or keeping a tidier locker room, people may wish to come up with their own criteria to figure out when they have achieved what they set out to do. In these cases, they might say they will try to compliment a teammate every single day or ask a coach for regular feedback on their locker room space.

A good goal is also meaningful. Because it is going to be something a person plans to dedicate their energy towards, it must align with their core values and interests. For athletes, working towards improvement in their sport is usually a very meaningful task because they love their sport and want to succeed. It is, however, important to keep in mind that while there might be many things an athlete wants to work towards, they might be limited in their ability to successfully do everything at once. When setting goals, they should decide which objectives are most important to them and then determine how much time and attention each individual goal requires. Then, they can choose which goals to focus on. Some athletes may aim for one big goal, while others may work toward several smaller goals. Taking on too much at once might make the athlete feel stressed, and they will not be able to put forth the effort they need to be successful.

A-Attainable and Actionable

The "A" in the SMART acronym stands for "attainable" and "actionable," which means the goal needs to be something that can realistically be achieved given an athlete's current skill and resources. It might be someone's dream to run a marathon, but if they have never done any long-distance running before, this is not a safe or realistic goal to try without training and first achieving a series of smaller goals. Instead, they might choose to start by running in some shorter community races and make the marathon something they work towards later on once they have started to develop their skills.

The goal must also be something an athlete can make happen for themselves, which means it needs to be about something they have control over. For example, "next season, I will have no early morning practices" is unrealistic, since an athlete rarely determines their own training schedule, usually this is up to coaches and team planners, so aiming for no early morning practices is more of a wish than a concrete goal! When it comes to training results, however, athletes have complete control over the effort they put forward and the extra work they do outside of team practice. Attainable and actionable goals are easier to work toward and therefore to achieve.

R–Realistic and Relevant

To be worthwhile, an athlete's goal must align with the bigger picture of what is happening in their lives. It must be realistic and relevant. First of all, it must be something they want to see themselves working towards. If they dislike lifting weights but make a goal to do it every day, they may not have the motivation it takes to follow through with their promise. If they change the goal to involve a different exercise they enjoy more or modify the one they have so that it is something they can see themselves doing, such as lifting weights with friends rather than going alone, it becomes much more realistic. People also need to consider how a certain goal fits with their other goals in other aspects of their lives and whether it is the right time in their lives to pursue them. If their objective requires them to train for six hours a day, they might not have time for it while they are in school, but it may be possible when they are on holiday.

T–Trackable and Time

Finally, all SMART goals should come with an estimate of how long it will take to achieve them. Athletes want to be sure they are giving themselves enough time to reasonably reach their goals, but not so much time they lose motivation. It may take weeks or months to attain the goals they are aiming for. For bigger goals, it can be helpful to break them up into small steps or pieces that can be reached more quickly to give people a sense of accomplishment while working towards their final targets. Competition and game days make excellent deadlines when making plans because they keep athletes accountable for their own progress.

TIPS FOR SETTING GOALS

Athletes may have a variety of goals they hope to achieve in their sport and in their lives. Some will take longer to reach than others. Many athletes like to start formulating their goals by starting to think about what they would like to achieve long-term, then narrowing their focus to more specific objectives they can meet along the way. By figuring out what their lifetime goals may be, athletes can determine the general direction they would like to work towards, which can shape their other decisions.

For athletes, lifetime goals may consist of the things they would like to accomplish by the end of their sports careers, or at least far into the foreseeable future. They may also wish to consider their goals in other areas of their life, including their educational, professional, family, and financial goals. This might help provide them with a picture of how their sport fits into their life as a whole, and whether their athletic goals align with everything else they are hoping to accomplish. Athletes can try brainstorming what is important to them, then narrow their focus to a couple of goals that are most important to them.

Whatever an athlete's goals may be, it is important that they are things the young person genuinely wants to achieve. It can be easy to make goals based on the opinions of parents and coaches. Often, athletes value what these people think and want to make them proud. Ultimately, the athlete is the one working towards them and living with the outcomes. If they do not feel their goals represent their true desires, they will not be happy and will feel less motivated when working towards them. People can and should consult with friends or family they trust when building their objectives, but ultimately, they must remain true to themselves and feel that their goals reflect their hopes and values.

These large lifetime goals can then be broken up into smaller goals. Athletes can plan what they would like to accomplish in the next five years, one year, six months, month, and week. They can break down their plans even further to make daily or weekly to-do lists that include tasks that get them closer to their end result. Each to-do list can build on the last, and these individuals can have confidence that whenever they cross something off, they are moving closer to their lifetime goals. Some people don't feel they need structured to-do lists, but having smaller goals gives them something to work towards in the short term and keeps them motivated to put in the effort they need to finally reach their lifetime objective.

It's important to remember that a person's lifetime goals, and even short-term goals, are not permanent. People change as they grow, learn new things, and have unexpected life changes. Their priorities may become different, and they may have more things they want to achieve. They may also learn things about themselves, and the factors they thought were most important to them no longer seem so significant. For example, a person may decide they no longer wish to compete in a sport but will continue to play simply because they enjoy it. This is very normal. Goals can be revisited as often as people need. Changing a goal because priorities change is not giving up, it is simply making adjustments that allow people to continue working towards the things that will make them happiest and most fulfilled.

Regardless of what type of goal they are setting and how long it will take them to achieve it, people should aim to write their goals down. They may wish to record it in a notes app or journal or turn it into a creative project such as a poster. This serves multiple purposes. One, it makes their goal feel real. Instead of just being a thought they focus on every once in a while, the goal becomes an actual phrase or image they can see and feel, which has a greater impact on them overall. It also serves as a reminder of what they are working towards. When their journey becomes difficult, or they feel they are not making progress, they can refer back to the original goal they made. Remember, this goal should be very specific and you should be able to describe it in detail.

Achieving a goal is always something to be proud of, no matter how big or small it may seem to others. Athletes deserve to celebrate their successes. They can share their wins with coaches, teammates, and family and may choose to reward themselves. In order to fulfill an objective, people need to overcome obstacles, and this takes commitment. It represents achieving something that was not possible before, and this is an incredible feat. With so many things to work toward in sport, it is tempting to brush aside small achievements as being insignificant and focus on other goals, but this diminishes an athlete's accomplishments. Take time to acknowledge your achievements, share your success, and feel proud of what you have worked for!

6

REBOOT HOW YOU THINK

While there is a lot that happens in our brains that we cannot see, one of the things we can become aware of and control are our thoughts. We are constantly thinking, forming judgments and opinions about the world around us, and planning our next move. Everything we do and say first starts in our mind as a thought. We filter some of these thoughts, edit others, and turn only a few into our final actions. It is not surprising that our thoughts play a major role in shaping our lives and the world we live in. By targeting what goes through our minds on a regular basis, we have incredible power to alter our performance.

Even the thoughts we never act on have tremendous power in the human mind. For one, they determine the environment in our brains. People who constantly think negative thoughts about themselves and others create a negative space in their minds. This is the space in which our subconscious learns and picks up on these negative cues. Because the subconscious mind aims to maintain homeostasis, it will usually default to bringing the person back to this negative headspace when it has the chance to do so. Thinking constructive thoughts allows the subconscious to learn how to foster positive behavior and keep a person feeling good.

Thoughts are also translated into words and actions, which other people notice. If we shape our words in a positive environment, they are more likely to be positive overall. When other people see us speaking and behaving constructively, they are more likely to echo this behavior and return the positivity right back to us. In this way, our positive thoughts will spark positivity in others and bring good things back to us.

Changing one's thought patterns might seem like an impossible task for a person. Ideas seem to just appear in the human mind, and very rarely is someone aware of them until they are completely formed. They often feel that they cannot control whether a particular thought they are having is positive or negative, it simply is. This is not necessarily true. Like many things we do, human beings often form thoughts based on habit, and it is possible to develop a habit of generating positive thinking patterns.

The first step in changing the way a person thinks is for them to notice their current state. It is difficult to know exactly what it is they would like to change and what their goals are if they do not currently know where they stand. People may wish to dedicate a certain amount of time every day to record the things that come to their minds. Keeping a journal or diary is often a great way to do this, or they might find they have an easier time just tuning into their thoughts every once in a while as they work through their daily tasks. In this stage, it is important to let thoughts come without judgment. We are simply noticing the things that come through our minds, not criticizing them.

After observing for a certain amount of time, athletes might be able to notice patterns in the way they think. They may have certain thoughts or themes that keep resurfacing. They might notice they are constantly critical of themselves or that they default to thinking of all the reasons why they might not be successful at something. They might be focused on mistakes they have made in the past, ones they are unable to change. These athletes might be picturing their future and all of the things that could go wrong in future competitions or practices. Whatever the case may be, if a thought keeps appearing in a person's mind, it is clearly important and deserves attention.

If the thoughts that keep coming up are consistently negative, these are worth thinking harder about and might need some attention to redirect them. In the beginning, it might seem impossible to redirect every single negative thought. In these cases, many people find it helpful to focus on one specific area or theme at a time. For example, if they are constantly having thoughts about not being "good enough" to succeed in their sport, they might choose to target these first and unpack the ideas whenever they appear.

WHEN NEGATIVE THOUGHTS APPEAR

No matter how hard we try, we will always have some negative thoughts that appear in our minds. When these do happen, it is important to not criticize ourselves for having them, but we do need to deal with them to prevent them from spiraling out of control. Negative thoughts have the most power when we pay attention to them. The more we focus on a thought, the more space it takes up in our minds and the bigger it grows. We want to make sure we are saving our space and attention for the positive things that are going to serve us well.

After recognizing a negative thought, one of the easiest things we can do to prevent it from taking over our brains is to redirect our minds. It does not matter what we redirect it to, as long as we take the focus away from the intrusive thought we had in the first place. We could think about what we ate for dinner last night, the plans we have for the weekend, or the way the sun looks during the day. As long as we refuse to engage with the negative thought, we are taking away its power.

It would be even better if we could consciously redirect our thoughts to something directly positive. We can think about something that makes us smile. It could be a funny joke or a compliment someone recently gave us. For example, we might choose to think about a friend or a family member we love or a place that makes us feel safe and happy. It can often be helpful to brainstorm a few "happy places" in advance so that when negative thoughts do appear, we immediately know where to redirect our minds.

While redirection works well for some people, others find it helpful to directly confront their thoughts. They take a moment to notice the thought, identify that it is unhelpful, and process it. It can often be nice to acknowledge that the negative things going through our minds are simply intrusive thoughts and nothing more. It is not fact, it is not an authority telling us something, it is our own minds that have created the statement. We can label the ideas as thoughts. Instead of telling ourselves "I am not good enough," we can say "I am awesome, I am amazing, I am perfect exactly as I am." This helps us distance ourselves from the negative idea. In addition, we can remind ourselves that "This is not real, it is just a thought. Negative thoughts only have power over me if I react to them."

We can then unpack these negative statements. Why did they come to mind? What was going on when the thought happened? Did we see or hear anything that put our minds in this space? In certain situations, we may have time to reflect on the thoughts we are having; in other circumstances, we might not have the time or capacity to do so. This is okay, simply acknowledging and distancing ourselves from negative thoughts is an excellent first step in creating a positive headspace.

In any case, regardless of whether or not we have had time to unpack what we are thinking, it's important to challenge negative thoughts by following up with a positive ones. This gives our minds something constructive to think about and gets us in the habit of forming ideas that make us feel good. If our thought is "I made a mistake, I'm not good enough," we can tell ourselves something like "I am learning and improving every day." Like any skill athletes learn, reframing thoughts in this way takes practice. They might find it takes a long time to come up with a positive alternative when they first begin to work on reframing their ideas, but rest assured that this does get easier with time.

Athletes must have faith they can rewire their minds. They are used to hard work and training. They know what commitment and practice are able to do. What is happening in an athlete's mind is entirely in their control. If they treat their thoughts like they do their bodies and dedicate time to training them, they will see incredible results.

As discussed earlier, affirmations can be another important tool to reinforce the power that positive thoughts can have. These are statements designed to train the subconscious mind and help program it into constructive habits. An affirmation that can be helpful in this instance is something like "my negative thoughts are weak; my positive thoughts are powerful." Athletes may create their own phrases that are meaningful to them and speak to their own subconscious minds. With time and repetition, the subconscious will learn the value of positive thoughts and come to give them the power they deserve in everyday life.

FOCUS ON CONTROL

One's thoughts are one thing that each individual has complete control over. They get to decide what they think and what occupies their attention, and because of this, their mindset is deserving of their time and attention. When we choose to dedicate our attention to the aspects of our life that we can control, we start taking full advantage of the power that lies within us. We embrace this power to make changes and form the life we most want to see. There will always be circumstances we cannot modify. Their outcomes are determined by other people or by factors in the world we cannot change. While it is tempting to become consumed by these circumstances, it is not always constructive. We can dedicate all of the energy we have toward fixating on the things we wish were different, but we will not change the outcome. Focusing on what we can control is a much better use of our mental resources.

One aspect of life that athletes are able to control is how they interact with their family members, coaches, and teammates in their lives. They choose who they surround themselves with and how they communicate with these people. Young athletes can decide to invest in their relationships by making time for those who matter most in their lives, and they can ask for help and support when they need it. They can make conscious choices to communicate honestly and respectfully, even if they are feeling tired, annoyed, or overwhelmed.

They can also decide to listen. Even though they might not know what another person is about to say, athletes can make space for their thoughts, requests, and opinions. It shows the other person in the relationship a level of respect by establishing that what they think is important and worth listening to. It also helps with the relationship as a whole. We don't often know what other people are thinking until they tell us. Instead of simply assuming something to be true, which we may do incorrectly, we can take the time to understand someone else's situation and respond appropriately.

What we cannot control is how these other people in our lives might act toward and communicate with us. Everyone makes their own decisions and chooses their own language in conversation. Occasionally, they may make choices that hurt us and make us feel disrespected. We cannot change that these decisions were made, but we can change how we react to them. If someone we love has done something to make us upset, we can let them know. It is not rude or accusatory to have this type of conversation; the goal is simply to tell the other person what the action was and how it made us feel. If they are someone important to us, it is most likely that they will want to know the effect their actions had and will be grateful for the opportunity to make amends. If we constantly feel upset by something another person is doing, we can make the decision to stop spending time around them. Everyone owes it to themselves to make choices that leave them feeling safe and respected. If there are people in their lives that do not make them feel this way, it is worth saving their time and energy for people who do.

People also have control over what happens in their free time. Athletes may not have much time to themselves due to their busy schedules, balancing school, training, and family commitments, but they can decide how to spend the time they do have. They can choose to do things that make them feel good, like volunteering or spending time with people they love. Young people can choose to be purposeful with their time. Rather than spending their days on their phones or watching television, they can make plans for other activities that bring them a sense of purpose and accomplishment. They can also decide to say no to commitments that do not bring them joy. If they have an offer to spend time with people who don't make them feel good or take part in an activity they don't particularly like, they can decline and spend their energy elsewhere.

Having a positive mindset and being mentally tough is not to say that bad things will not happen. Everyone has losses, disappointments, and failures. This is not something anyone is able to change. What people do have control over is how they react to these situations. They can let disappointments become negative thoughts that spiral and intensify mental health struggles, or they can choose to move forward and leave the disappointment behind. They can think about what went wrong and learn from it, but they do not need to live in the past. Once a mistake has been made, it has already happened. The future, however, has not and contains so many opportunities for improvement. What an individual gets to decide is whether their disappointments will defeat them, or whether they will motivate them.

When something does happen, individuals get to decide whether they will react or respond to the situation. A reaction is usually immediate. It is a decision people make based on their emotions rather than their logical thoughts, and it is usually impulsive. People who tend to react to negative situations often don't analyze the implications of their actions and how they might impact their futures. On the other hand, when something happens, people may also respond. A response is usually more purposeful and measured than a reaction. People who respond take time to process their emotions, think through the different options available to them and calculate their course of action. They are usually happier with the outcomes of their decisions because they have had more time to think them through.

Athletes can take back some control over negative situations they might find themselves in by choosing to respond to them rather than react. They can make a point of taking time before important decisions in emotionally-charged situations. It's okay for people to ask for time when they need it to allow themselves space to process their emotions and make decisions rationally rather than impulsively. They may also wish to talk through things with people they trust and hear the opinions of friends or family before committing to any one course of action. In any case, taking this time allows athletes to remain in control rather than letting immediate, emotional reactions take charge.

How one reacts to failures is often a tribute to an individual's mindset. Those with a growth mindset often see mistakes as a stepping stone toward overall improvement. They believe their potential is unlimited and that with dedication and hard work, they can achieve anything they want. People with a fixed mindset, on the other hand, believe that they are born with all of the talent and intelligence they will ever have.

They feel they cannot mold their brains with exercises and learning opportunities and that they simply need to make do with what they have already been given in life. These are the people who tend to be more afraid of trying new things for fear of failure. In reality, failure is a normal part of learning new skills. Those with a growth mindset often react better when things don't go according to their original plans and are able to use their mistakes to push their skills farther than those with fixed mindsets.

Athletes also have complete control of how they look after their bodies. They decide what they eat, how much they sleep, and what time they dedicate to exercise. People always feel better if they have good, healthy habits; if they start to deprive themselves of the things they need to thrive, like sleep and proper nutrition, their physical and mental health both suffer. Young people can exercise control in their own lives by caring for themselves and making their physical health a priority. Their mental health will benefit greatly as a result.

Finally, and most importantly, athletes are able to control when they ask for help. There are times when they may feel overwhelmed or like they don't have any power at all. They might be anxious, depressed, or burnt out. In many cases, people in these situations shut down or withdraw from others, making it difficult to reclaim their control. When this happens, it is important for athletes to realize what is going on in their lives and advocate for themselves. They can connect with a teammate, coach, or family member to explain how they are feeling and ask for support. These are people who care about the athlete's well-being and genuinely want to see them succeed. They will be able to offer the support they can and help the athlete find resources to provide anything extra they might need. Involving other people is not an athlete giving up control of their situation, it is recruiting more people to their support team and reclaiming ownership of what is happening.

The way people think and the things they choose to focus on are habits, like any other. Just like how an athlete becomes used to brushing their teeth every day or drinking water before a big game, they get used to certain patterns of thinking. Habits are established by repetition and reinforcement. The more an athlete trains themselves to think a certain way, the more they will think that way on their own. When they notice they are thinking in a way that is not constructive, they can avoid the habit of unhelpful thinking by correcting their mindset right away and introducing positive thoughts instead. If they don't make this adjustment, they run the risk of teaching themselves bad habits. For people who are committed to rebooting their minds, it is important to constantly think about the ideas that are coming into their heads and commit to building good habits.

The human mind is a very powerful organ that has the ability to shape the world we live in. Our thoughts affect how we act and feel, while our conscious focus determines how we build our lives. Athletes can train their minds, like they do their bodies, to have positive thoughts that serve them well and focus on the things in their worlds that they can control. This will help them embrace positive thinking and set themselves up for success, both inside and outside the world of sport.

7

VISUALIZATION

Many athletes have often pictured the victories they hope to achieve. They see movies in their minds of what they might look like when they cross a finish line or score a winning goal. They can already feel the pride in their hearts from the victory and cannot wait until it becomes reality. It helps motivate them to train. They want to turn the world that exists in their imagination into reality. What many people do not know, however, is that imagining their world in this way can be a powerful tool that helps them on their road to success. This is a process called visualization.

Visualization is a technique that consists of picturing something in the mind before it becomes reality, and it has been consciously and deliberately employed by athletes all across the world since the 1980s. People can use this technique to prepare themselves for a specific event, such as a presentation or competition, or they can use it to picture their goals. They can outline in their mind exactly how they would like their situation to play out. They can picture what it will smell like, how it will feel, and what they will be thinking in order to completely immerse themselves into their imagined state. Their minds are working hard, but their bodies are completely relaxed. Although it might seem that everything is in their head, many people find they experience real results from regular and thorough visualization, making it a practice that athletes may wish to adopt for themselves.

Some professional athletes, including Olympic swimmer Michael Phelps, swear by this strategy. According to a 2016 interview with his coach, Phelps uses visualization for two hours a day starting months before an important race (Headspace, 2022). He thinks through every important detail and uses all of his senses to create a complete picture of what the big day will feel like. One study examined the effects of visualization on people who were asked to regularly picture workouts, and found that those who did so regularly were actually able to build muscle (Headspace, 2022). In fact, people who simply visualized their exercises were able to build almost half as much muscle as the people who did them in real life (Headspace, 2022). This demonstrates how a person's brain can impact how their body develops and by influencing their thoughts with visualization, they can see real results.

This practice can also be associated with decreased anxiety, especially when it comes to events and performances. By picturing a moment or competition over and over again, a person becomes more familiar with it. They get used to the little details they can expect to encounter and feel more at home in their situation. They might also have the opportunity to think through the types of problems they may encounter and come up with potential solutions to help them feel more prepared. This way, when they go to perform in real life, they are no longer navigating the competition for the first time and can be more relaxed. Often, when people are less stressed, they have an easier time thinking and are more likely to perform better.

The human brain responds very well to visual stimuli, and sometimes it has trouble differentiating between things it has experienced in real life and something it has only seen in a visualization session. By using regular visualization, people are able to convince their minds that they have experienced something before. In particular, they retrain the structure in the brain most responsible for the fight-or-flight stress response, known as the amygdala. If a situation seems familiar to them when it actually takes place, their amygdala is less likely to initiate an automatic reaction and kick-start the stress response in their body.

People who regularly use visualization may also experience increased focus on competition day. At a sporting event, there are a lot of details to consider and distractions that come up. Some of these are logistical challenges involved with registering for the event, some involve the people in the audience, and others might be thoughts that simply run through an athlete's mind the day of the big event. These can take away from an athlete's ability to concentrate and do their best. By conducting repeated visualization exercises, people are able to identify the details that are most important to focus on and train their brains to zero in on them, making it easier to concentrate on their performance.

Finally, regular visualization has the ability to boost a person's confidence. Imagining themselves achieving their goals in such vivid detail can help them believe it is possible. It allows them to see their victories and plan exactly how to get there. They develop more faith in their abilities and, because they have seen themselves win in their imagination, they look forward to winning in real life.

USING VISUALIZATION

There are several different visualization techniques athletes can experiment with to find the ones that work best for them. They can aim to set aside time every day to dedicate to this practice. It does not need to be a lot of time, but it should be something they can regularly commit to. Even taking a few minutes in the morning after they wake up or in the evening on their way to bed can make an incredible impact on the way they feel. These are often great times because this is when the individual is most likely to be relaxed and ready to let visualizations come into their mind. It's important for a person to choose a quiet location for visualizations to take place and minimize distractions where possible. This will allow them to focus on the task at hand and feel most comfortable in their environment.

Some people like to picture a big event taking place, almost like a movie. They imagine their ideal scenario playing out perfectly, with every detail accounted for. They take the time to think about the people who are there with them, the weather, the clothing they are wearing, and the sounds in the environment. The person may then wish to imagine themselves stepping into the world they have established. By doing this, they are making the conscious choice to insert themselves into their perfect world and accept the reality as their own. They can picture themselves making good things happen. People can then picture themselves stepping back out of the movie, folding it up, and taking it with them so that it travels wherever they need to go.

Others like to create tangible visual images to help themselves picture achieving their goals. They can take pictures of places they would like to be, or find them on the internet, and insert themselves by either cutting and pasting their own picture or using a computer program to modify it digitally. For example, if an athlete would like to one day win an Olympic medal, they can create a photograph of themselves on a podium or in an Olympic stadium. They can keep these photos somewhere important, like on a vision board or in an album on their phone, so they can refer to them whenever they feel they need a reminder of what they are working towards.

Whatever it is that an athlete wants to manifest into reality, there is a good chance it can be turned into a visualization. One of the most popular images people tend to create is that of themselves achieving a goal or personal victory. For many athletes, this looks like winning a competition. They might see themselves at a championship game or finishing an important race that will win them a prize. In any case, their visualization should involve the team they are with, the details they will focus on, and the strategies they plan on using to win.

It is also worthwhile to use visualization as a strategy when learning how to cope with stress. When they are feeling anxious or overwhelmed, many people will simply react and make decisions based on their emotions. Often these decisions are things that get them out of uncomfortable situations, which is a protective reflex human beings are programmed for. However, when people are not in immediate danger, it's often best to think through decisions and not jump right to any one response.

For people who wish to use visualizations to help them learn how to perform under this type of pressure, it can often be useful to think about all the anxious moments they have had recently and play them out differently in their minds. They can picture themselves dealing with issues and then imagine positive outcomes. These visualizations can help athletes picture a reality where they are in complete control of their emotions and the world around them. They can help people feel powerful, like they have the ability to shape situations how they would like. Athletes can also practice strategies like deep breathing, which help calm their immediate stress responses and allow them to focus on what is most important to the situation.

While visualizations can be incredibly useful for picturing the outcome of a single problem or event, they do not need to be specific to just that one thing. They can be used to picture a world where everything is well-balanced and stressors from all areas of their lives are under control. They can picture themselves passing their exams successfully, meeting all family commitments, and training well for their sport. They can see a place where they have time to accomplish everything that is important to them and look after both their physical and mental health. It can be helpful to explore single events in detail, but it can be just as rewarding to use visualization as a tool to figure out where these events fit into a person's life as a whole.

There is so much that can be gained from simply visualizing the future an individual wants to see for themselves. Practicing regular visualizations has the potential to help athletes improve their performance, relieve stress, and focus on what is most important to them. People may choose different strategies for visualizations, but all involve inserting themselves into the world they most want to create. Once established in their mind, an athlete's vision for success becomes easier to achieve.

8

MEDITATION AND BREATH WORK

Meditation and breath work are other strategies athletes may wish to use when coping with stress and optimizing their mental health. When incorporated into their daily routines, it can help them build mental toughness and give them tools they can fall back on when they feel particularly overwhelmed. There are multiple ways in which an athlete can approach meditation and breath work; this chapter will outline just a few.

MEDITATION

For thousands of years, meditation has been used in many different forms in religious practices, including in Buddhism, Christianity, and Hinduism. This practice became more commonplace in North America in the 1960s and has since been embraced by people looking to take advantage of the benefits it offers. More recently, it has been adopted as a psychotherapy tool for managing mental health.

Although there are different types of meditation, all come down to simply focusing one's attention and noticing the world around them. When meditating, a person places themselves in the position of a passive observer. They do not make judgments about what they see or analyze their observations, they just let them happen. They become aware of their thoughts but do not criticize themselves for having them or engage with these thoughts.

One type of mediation, concentrative meditation, is a practice that involves focusing one's attention on something specific. This can be a physical object they look at, like an artifact they are holding, or a focal point in the distance. It can also be a phrase or mantra they repeat over and over again, noticing how it sounds and how the words make them feel. Having something to direct their attention to often helps people clear their minds of chaos and allows them to live in the present.

Another popular form of meditation is known as mindfulness meditation. It involves a person noticing the environment they are in. They pay attention to the sights, sounds, and smells that surround them. They become aware of the feelings inside of their body, including feelings in their stomach or tension in their muscles. In this type of practice, people strive to notice the support from the chair underneath them or the pressure of the ground beneath their feet. They notice the way their clothes feel and the way their breath moves in and out of their lungs. In this form of meditation, people only focus on what is happening at the current moment, and often they pay attention to things they would not otherwise notice.

Mindfulness meditation can also be practiced using a "body scan" technique. In this practice, a person shifts their focus from one part of their body to another so that they may pay attention to the things they feel at each point. It's often best to work systematically to ensure no parts of the body are forgotten, and the practice flows from one location to another. If someone notices they have any tension in a part of their body, they can take the opportunity to take a deep breath and relax their muscles. For example, someone may decide to start their "body scan" at their head. They might notice the way the air feels on their skin, whether they are wearing a hat, and any tension in their facial muscles. Once they feel they have given enough attention to this region, they can move on and focus on their neck or upper back. They should continue to work like this until they reach their toes, at which point their practice will be complete.

There are also several guided meditation sessions that can be accessed online at no cost through sites such as YouTube or via mobile applications. They come in various lengths and formats, which means interested athletes can find one that suits their own personal preferences. Certain people prefer to use these guided sessions while they are first establishing their practice to help them explore strategies they might like to use and hold them accountable. There is no one "right" way to meditate; athletes who are interested in incorporating this into their lives can experiment with several different strategies until they find one that is a good fit for them.

During their meditation session, a person aims to clear their mind and does not think about anything they might have to deal with outside of the session itself. Their goal is to keep themselves in the present moment; the past and future are things that can be focused on later. They do not think about work, school, or family life if they can help it, although occasionally these thoughts might find them. Instead, their focus remains on the meditation until it is complete.

The goal of the practice, however, is not for a person to shut themselves off completely to these unrelated thoughts. When they do appear, which is often the case when the mind is allowed to wander, people do not need to banish them right away. They are allowed to notice them, let the thought sit, and have it disappear in its own time. The mind is kept open so that the thoughts may escape and ensure nothing is latching onto them to make them stay. When the mind engages with a thought, it fixates on it and causes it to grow. It becomes the mind's focus, rather than the meditation at hand. By creating a headspace that allows these thoughts the freedom to escape, a person is able to redirect their attention to their present state and return to their practice.

Feeling emotions during a meditation session is also natural. People should allow themselves to feel joy, sadness, grief, confusion, or any other feelings that arise. These might be prompted by thoughts that come to mind, or by simply having the time and space to exist without distraction. When people feel such things, it's important to acknowledge them and, like with thoughts, let them pass in their own time. Feelings come to a person's attention because they need to be processed, and meditation is often a great way to create a space for them to exist.

Like any other skill, having a clear mind and reclaiming focus after intrusive thoughts are things that get easier to do with time. Many people find that when they first start meditation, they frequently have to bring themselves back to the present because their mind wanders away from the practice at hand. Their brains are full of observations, to-do lists, and thoughts about events that have already passed. As soon as they have a quiet moment in their busy lives, their mind tries to fill the silence. What they often find is that once they have been practicing for an extended period of time, they become used to the feeling of being in the present and know how to navigate their own brain. They are able to practice for longer sessions at a time and start feeling the positive effects that come from regular meditation.

For athletes interested in trying meditation, it can often be easiest to start with small sessions and work their way up to a longer practice. Even committing to five minutes of focused meditation every day can have incredible benefits. It can feel less overwhelming to commit to smaller sessions, and they often fit more easily into busy schedules. If the idea of practicing is not overwhelming, athletes are more likely to follow through with having regular sessions rather than putting off the practice or giving up entirely. Some people like to set timers before they begin to ensure they do not need to interrupt their practice to check a clock.

It is also important to choose a suitable location for meditating. Athletes can take whatever position they would like, as long as they feel safe and comfortable. Whatever they choose needs to be something that allows them to relax. If they are uncomfortable, it will take some of their focus away from their practice. Meditation works best when there are minimal distractions. Any room where the individual is able to close a door to separate themselves from regular household noise is often ideal.

Benefits of Meditation

For many people, meditating is a calming activity that can help them feel more relaxed as they go about their day. By clearing their minds and purposefully redirecting their attention, people are able to give themselves a break from the stressors they experience in their everyday lives. They can also separate themselves from distressing thoughts they keep fixating on, which gives them an opportunity to let them go. Research has shown that meditation practice can decrease heart rate, lower respiration rate, and change brain wave patterns, all of which are associated with a reduction of stress (Cherry, 2020). This can make meditation a great tool to use if an athlete needs to take a break from an overwhelming situation or prepare themselves to think clearly. It can also make this practice an excellent tool for relieving symptoms of anxiety and depression in certain individuals.

In addition to this, meditation can be used to help ease sleep disorders and encourage good quality sleep. When people experience stress, their body prepares to fight it, which means their ability to rest becomes impaired. They are alert in case of potential danger, which means sleep is not an option. By bringing themselves into a more relaxed state, people are more likely to fall asleep faster.

Regular practice has also been linked with a greater sense of self-awareness. By spending time noticing the thoughts and feelings they experience on a day-to-day basis, people learn about themselves. They pay attention to their emotional state, which might help tell them what they need at a given moment. These people also gain practice identifying and naming certain feelings, which means they are able to pick up on them when they come up outside of their meditation sessions.

BREATH WORK

Our breath is very closely linked with our emotions. Many people will notice that when they are excited or nervous, they take short, sharp breaths. When they first wake up in the morning and are in a relaxed state, their breaths are slower and longer. By encouraging these slow, long breaths, athletes can help themselves adopt a more relaxed state of being. This is where the concept of breath work comes into play. Like with meditation, there are several different approaches an athlete can use if they would like to start using breath work as a tool in their everyday lives, and they might find some strategies work better for them than others.

One common strategy that has been used since the 1950s is known as Buteyko breathing. This is a practice that involves drawing and holding a series of breaths to improve a person's ability to control the way air moves in and out of their body. Some studies have linked this particular strategy with a decrease in asthma symptoms as well as problems with the Eustachian tube, which is part of the middle ear (Wilson, 2021). It can also help people stabilize their breathing patterns, preventing hyperventilation and reducing anxiety.

Certain instructors that teach Buteyko breathing recommend practicing for 15-20 minutes every day; however, any amount of time can help athletes practice their breath control (Wilson, 2021). They recommend taking a comfortable position sitting on the floor or on a chair using good upright posture. People taking this position should strive to have their shoulders back and their spine elongated, stretching up towards the ceiling. They can then take a minute to breathe normally, however that might look like for them on that particular day.

Next, the person breathing will engage in a series of controlled pauses. After an exhalation, they will hold their breath, plugging their nose with their fingers until they feel the need to breathe in again. They will then release their nose, take a breath and allow themselves to breathe normally once again for at least 10 seconds. They can repeat this process over and over as many times as they would like.

After several controlled pauses, a person can then move on to maximum pauses. After exhaling, they will once again hold their breath and plug their nose, but they will do so for a longer period of time. Their goal will be to hold their breath for as long as possible, which is often twice the length of their controlled pause. When they are at the point of moderate discomfort, they can inhale again and return to normal breathing. This process can also be repeated as many times as desired.

Another popular breathing technique some athletes might like to use, especially during times of stress, is called pursed lip breathing. This is where a person presses their lips tight together, except for one small o-shaped opening at the front of their mouth. They can then focus on bringing air in and out through this hole, almost as if they were breathing through a straw. This helps control the amount of air a person can bring in and out of their body at once, which forces them to take longer, slower breaths. A technique like this one can prevent people from hyperventilating and return their breathing to a normal resting pattern.

One final technique that can be helpful is known as belly breathing. In this pattern, a person imagines themselves breathing all the way down into their abdomen. Rather than focusing on having their chest rise and fall, they should expect to see their belly moving up and down with each breath. This visual can often encourage a person to breathe deeply and calm their nervous system. It can also allow them to slow their breathing. If they picture air traveling all the way down their body, it has further to move than it would if it simply stopped in the person's chest. This means the person will imagine the air taking longer to get where it needs to be, causing their breathing pattern to slow.

When using breathing techniques like these, it is important for athletes to check in with themselves frequently and pay attention to how they are feeling. If at any point, they feel anxious, unwell, or light-headed, they should pause their breath work and return to normal breathing until they feel comfortable once again. If they have heart issues, high blood pressure, or another serious medical condition, they should avoid breath work exercises altogether until they have spoken with a health care professional about whether or not this is something they will be able to do safely.

Meditation and breath work are incredibly powerful tools that athletes can use at almost anytime to relax and manage their stress. They may wish to experiment with different techniques until they find one that works for them. Both of these practices have incredible physical and mental health benefits, and when used regularly, promise to bring mental toughness to athletes who choose to use them.

9

GRATITUDE

Another simple practice that can have dramatic results is making gratitude into a habit. Practicing gratitude means that a person takes a moment to appreciate the things in their lives that serve them well. These can be practical things, like having access to food and water, or they can be more frivolous things, like a good vacation. No matter who they are or what their level is, every athlete has positive things in their lives they can be thankful for. Whether this is having supportive teammates or even just the opportunity to play the sport itself, reflecting on these things can be incredibly beneficial. This is a practice that can happen anytime and anywhere, regardless of where an athlete may be.

As human beings, we are often hard-wired into negative thinking. We spend time analyzing our mistakes and what is lacking in our lives. Our friends and neighbors might have things we do not, and we feel jealous as a result. People spend time considering the awards they would like to get, things they would like to buy, and experiences they would like to have. They are always looking into the future at what could be and only see what is lacking from their current lives.

Athletes in particular are often susceptible to this. They are frequently goal-oriented individuals who strive for constant improvement. These are people who train constantly to upgrade their strengths and skills. They look up to coaches and other athletes as examples of what they could be one day. When they lose a competition, they often feel disappointed and come up with strategies that could bring them to victory the next time they compete. Athletes are programmed to see what is missing from their own skills and look to the future for opportunities to improve them. In all of this, they can sometimes forget to be grateful for what they do have.

When people are stuck thinking about all the things they are missing in life, they can often feel upset by what they do not have. They might feel inadequate for not achieving certain milestones or jealous because they don't have certain material objects. This can leave them with a negative mindset. Gratitude can help people become more aware of the things that are going well in their lives. It can shift their mindset from focusing on all of the things they don't have to the things they do have, which is often more things than they may be aware of.

Being grateful for the things in their lives, however, does not mean that a person stops seeing the potential in their future. They can still work toward their goals and acknowledge when they have areas that need improvement. Multiple things can be true at once. A person can be thankful for the skills they have but still have a goal to work towards in the future. The key is for athletes to think of their goals as opportunities rather than things that are lacking in their lives. They see the opportunity as something they already have, and possibly even something to be thankful for, and they don't make themselves feel bad for not having already achieved the milestone. These athletes recognize that they will always have goals to work towards but remain proud of what they have already done.

Practicing gratitude also does not diminish the fact that sometimes, difficult things happen in life and in sport. These disappointments will always be difficult to deal with, and it is okay to feel all of the emotions that come with them. Sadness, frustration, and anger are all healthy, and athletes often need to process these emotions as part of moving on from the negative experience. What gratitude aims to do is build up the positive things that do happen and give athletes a break from dwelling on what did not go right. It is not meant to make someone abandon their disappointment, but rather to help them see the full picture of what their lives are like. Positive things can be difficult to appreciate when a person is in a negative headspace, but gratitude can help bring them to light.

Although it is a simple concept, taking the time to be thankful for important things in life can have some surprisingly significant benefits. In one study conducted by researchers at the University of Miami, participants were asked to write a few sentences each week. Some were tasked with writing things they were grateful for, some identified things that irritated them, and others simply identified events from their week without noting if they were positive or negative. After 10 weeks of reflection, the people who wrote about the things they were thankful for reported feeling better about their lives (Harvard Medical School, 2021). Interestingly, the researchers in this study also found these people visited doctors less and exercised more, implying that their practice might have had some physical health benefits as well.

Other studies have also found that gratitude can have an impact on a person's relationships. Couples who regularly take time to express feelings of gratitude often report feeling more positive towards each other (Harvard Medical School, 2021). These people are also more likely to feel they can bring up difficulties in their relationship if something concerns them. While these studies are generally limited to people in romantic relationships, it is likely that people in friendships or professional relationships can reap similar benefits by expressing appreciation for others.

ESTABLISHING A PRACTICE

Whether a person decides to establish a regular practice involving gratitude or simply make an effort to add more moments of thanks to their everyday lives, they will experience similar benefits. A lot of people prefer to work gratitude into their daily schedules to help it become a habit and ensure they do not forget about it. Many will take time in the morning to be thankful, to ensure they start each day on a positive note, or they will practice gratitude before they fall asleep so that they can consider and appreciate the events that happened during their day.

For people who want to make a regular habit of being thankful, an easy way to start is to make a list of things that they appreciate in their lives. These can be significant life events, such as being accepted into a university or winning a sports competition, or they can be small daily occurrences, like putting on a favorite sweater. A person can leave these things as thoughts, but they can also say them out loud or record them on paper or on their phone. Writing down the things they are grateful for is often incredibly helpful because statements can feel more real when people can physically see them and connect with them.

It is perfectly acceptable for a person to repeat their statements of gratitude multiple days in a row, especially if they are about something that has a strong presence in their lives. They should make it a goal, however, to include some more specific statements that are relevant to their daily lives. This encourages them to think about what it is they would like to acknowledge in their practice, rather than falling into the habit of repeating the same few statements. Gratitude is more meaningful when it comes with genuine reflection and appreciation. Rather than simply saying "I am thankful for the opportunity to play my sport," an athlete may decide to make their statement more specific by saying something like "I enjoyed practice today, I am thankful for my teammate who helped make it so much fun." This takes a general statement, which may still hold true, and frames it with regard to the events of that day.

An interesting thing often happens when people commit to finding a handful of things they appreciate. They start becoming more aware of the things that make them happy as they happen. Knowing they will need to think of something later for their gratitude practice, they pay more attention to positive things in their world and make mental notes so they can recall them later. In other words, people go looking for reasons to be happy, which helps them be in a more positive headspace overall.

Another way athletes can practice gratitude is by thanking the people in their lives who do things for them. They can thank a friend who did them a favor, a family member who took care of them, or a coach who gave them good advice. They may choose to thank the person face-to-face or write a thank-you card that can be given at a later time. Not only will this practice help the athlete experience the benefits of gratitude, but it will also help the other important people in their world feel good too. These people might be touched to learn the impact their actions had on the athlete and feel happy they were able to make a difference. They might also be more likely to repeat their actions to help the athlete again or do a similar favor for someone else.

For athletes who are religious, prayer can be an important way to practice gratitude. A lot of religions have practices that focus on appreciating the good things in life. This might involve having someone directly say words to articulate how they are feeling, or they might simply sit with their thoughts and appreciate the world around them. Whether they practice alone or in a church or prayer group, someone who prays regularly can experience a lot of the same benefits as those who create their own gratitude program. If prayer is important to an athlete, regularly making time for it in their schedule can help bring them a positive mindset.

No matter what an athlete chooses to do when they practice gratitude, it's important that when they state they are thankful for something, they mean it. If they claim to be thankful for things they do not really appreciate, their statements will feel false, even if it is something they think they are supposed to be thankful for. The practice will not be a genuine reflection but will instead just involve "going through the motions" of gratitude. The athlete will not get the same benefits as they would if their practice was genuine.

If the athlete feels they should be thankful for something, but they are, in fact, not, this might be an opportunity for more reflection. Perhaps they feel they should be thankful for their part-time job but inside they feel it is more of an inconvenience than an opportunity. The work environment may not be quite right for them, or they may not get along with their coworkers. In this case, if there is nothing that makes them feel thankful for their job, it might be a sign they need to consider whether or not this is a positive thing in their life. They may need to think about suggesting modifications at work that make their job a better place for them or finding a new job altogether. In any case, telling themselves they are thankful for their job is not going to help them feel happier.

Sometimes, people may feel that they don't have anything to be grateful for. They might be having a bad week or are upset about something they can't control. This can be an obstacle to practicing gratitude and for many, this is the reason they choose not to practice altogether. If an athlete feels like this on a particular day but is still interested in continuing their practice, they can come up with simple statements about things in their lives. On days like these, it is more important than ever to continue finding things to be thankful for. A person may need to think harder about positive things that have happened to them. Beautiful weather or a good cup of coffee are excellent things to appreciate. Even something as simple as "I'm grateful I am alive" still counts as practicing and can serve as a good reminder of the good things that exist in difficult times.

Gratitude can also be an excellent team activity. After a competition or practice, have team members gather and name one thing they are particularly grateful for. This can be a wonderful and affirming ritual. These things may or may not be related to the sport. Multiple people may have the same thing they are appreciative of, and this is okay! By having each person contribute a positive, constructive thought, the team will be able to fill their space with positive feelings and all be able to take advantage of the benefits of the practice of gratitude. It can also be helpful to hear what other people in their lives are thankful for to learn a little more about them and uncover more positivity in the world.

With all of the chaos that can exist in a young athlete's busy schedule, it is important for them to remember to take time to appreciate the positive things in their lives. These can be people, places, or opportunities that bring them joy and allow them to be successful. There are several different ways a person can practice gratitude, and for those who make a point of doing this, there can be incredible benefits that can go a long way when establishing mental toughness.

10

FINDING THE RIGHT BALANCE

While sports are certainly important for young athletes, they are just one component of a busy life. Young people often have classes, part-time jobs, family commitments, and other extracurricular activities they need to attend to. These are all excellent things that can provide so many opportunities for young people to learn new skills and meet friends that will last a lifetime. However, when someone reaches a competitive level in their sport, it can feel like it begins to take up all of their time. In reality, people need a variety of different experiences to live full lives, and the key is to try to find a way to balance everything that needs to be done. Finding the right balance will ensure young athletes get to have all of the experiences that are most important to them while still dedicating time and attention toward training for their sport.

It can be tempting to think that being a world-class athlete requires that someone gives 100% of their time and effort to their sport all the time. The media often talks about the "grind" and praises athletes who work themselves to exhaustion. There is a mindset in competitive sports that says if a person is not constantly pushing through pain, they are not making progress. This can force an athlete to continue working even once they are physically and mentally exhausted.

Many coaches and competitive leagues might also make scheduling difficult for their athletes. Some competitive organizations will expect their members to prioritize their sport over everything else in their lives. They will bench an athlete for skipping practices, even if it is for attending important school or family events. Practices may start early in the morning or end late in the evening, which can make it difficult for a young person to get the sleep they need to remain healthy. In addition, practices take up hours every day, and between training, travel, competition, reviewing game film, and volunteering for the team, athletes are left with very little free time of their own.

One common experience for young athletes is having the feeling that they are constantly saying "I can't, I have practice" when asked to make plans. They often have the sense that they are missing out on family functions or opportunities to visit with friends because of their aggressive sports schedules. These people may not be familiar with the world of sports and may not understand the commitment the athlete has already made to their team. The young person may frequently feel bad when they have to decline plans and this may lead them to have negative feelings about their sport.

These extra plans with friends and family are important, and so are all of the other things athletes would like to accomplish in their lives. Social time outside of a sports team is what allows young athletes to build support networks and develop well-rounded interests. It is what can make them feel like a whole person rather than just an athlete. This is important because it helps young people develop a sense of self and can allow them to do meaningful things even once they are finished competing in their chosen sport.

TIPS FOR FINDING BALANCE

Planning is critical for any athlete looking to juggle multiple commitments with the demands of competitive sports. While spontaneously deciding to do something might be fun, it is usually not an option for people who already have busy schedules. Tools like agendas can make all the difference for young athletes. Students can purchase these from office supply stores, or they can ask their schools if they have any they are giving away. Some institutions provide planners free of charge to interested students; often they will even have important school events already printed inside. Students can use these to plan out all of their important commitments weeks in advance and see, at a glance, what time they have available for extra things. Athletes often find it helpful to book off practice time, mark assignment due dates, and pencil in important family functions such as birthday and anniversary parties.

Online calendars can also make great planning tools. Most computers and smartphones have a calendar function already programmed into their software. Athletes can add important events electronically and be reminded before they start. They might even be able to program recurring functions, which can be an excellent time saver. For example, if the athlete knows they have practice every Tuesday night, they can set their calendars to book off a segment of time for that event every week. Athletes should make sure they stay on top of their planners, add new commitments when they become aware of them, and remove ones that are no longer relevant to their lives.

However, scheduling can feel like a logistical puzzle. Every commitment has to fit somewhere, but it is not always obvious where each one is meant to go. One strategy that some athletes find helpful is scheduling major time commitments first. If there are things that absolutely cannot be moved, like competition days, they can be added to the calendar before anything else. Then, time-consuming events can be added because they will be the most difficult to schedule. Things that take less time or that can be broken up into several smaller events, like household chores, can be scheduled last to help them fit around everything that is already in place. Athletes should be sure they account for travel time to and from their commitments so that they are not surprised when they need to move around.

One major benefit of scheduling is the fact that it allows athletes to work far in advance. Almost every student is familiar with the feeling of having an assignment due and not enough time to complete it. Maybe they procrastinated until the last minute, or maybe they had more work than they thought. Either way, they are up late at night in a panic-fuelled working frenzy, frantically trying to put something together. Not only is this incredibly stressful, but it does not allow a person to do their best possible work. Inevitably, they will forget to include some details or not have enough time to proofread their work, which will affect the grade they earn.

By keeping a regular planner, students can make sure they never forget a deadline. They will not be surprised with tests and assignments they need to work through at the last minute. These people will be able to see what they are supposed to get done and come up with a strategy of how to do it that works around their other commitments. They may even create timelines that break down the work they are supposed to do. This way, students can spread out their studying so that they don't need to complete it all at once. For example, if they are preparing for an exam, they may decide to study one chapter from their textbook every day for one week before the test. If they are writing an essay, they may draft one page or topic of their paper every day until it is complete. People should also remember to include time for proofreading their papers or practicing their presentations when planning their work timelines.

Athletes should also make a habit of making effective use of their free time. In many cases, athletes find themselves doing a lot of waiting on competition days. They often have travel time on a team bus, wait to become registered for the competition, and wait while other athletes have their turn to race or play. All of these gaps in their schedule can be excellent opportunities for schoolwork. Young people may be able to bring notes or assignments to their competitions and see how much progress they can make during their "downtime." If they get a lot of work done, they will have more time later for relaxing.

Even if they do not have work due in the immediate future, athletes should aim to work ahead as much as they can. They might choose to start an essay that is due in a few weeks or begin making flashcards for their final exam well in advance. This way, they will be prepared in case something comes up at the last minute and they cannot do as much work as they initially intended. It can also help reduce their stress levels. If athletes complete assignments early, they can get them "off of their plate" and stop thinking about them. They will be able to enjoy their team practices and social time more because they will not be worrying about when they will get their work finished.

Part of young people's task of staying ahead of their schoolwork is checking in with themselves often to determine what they do and do not understand. When they do not understand a certain concept, they should aim to clarify it as much as possible. Especially as they advance to later years of study, class concepts often build on one another. The things an athlete learns are not only important for their current tests and assignments, but they will also help them understand concepts they will learn down the road. If they have something they do not understand, they will be lost later and will end up spending more time and energy trying to catch up.

When they do find something they are struggling with, students can spend some time with their study resources, like their textbooks, to try and learn more about it. Sometimes, however, it can be difficult for a person to clarify a concept on their own. They may wish to seek help from classmates or teachers or recruit the help of a tutor. Athletes should see what is available to them through their school or sports league. Some organizations have connections with free tutoring services young people can take advantage of. Tutors have an excellent understanding of the concepts they are teaching and often take training courses that help them explain ideas well. They will certainly be helpful resources for young people who need them.

It is also incredibly important that athletes make time to rest. If they are focused on scheduling their time using a planner, it can be tempting to feel that they must always be taking part in an organized activity in order to be productive. This is not always the case. The word "productive" simply means an individual is accomplishing something important. Resting is very important! Just because they aren't busy doing some structured activity does not mean the individual isn't doing something of value. They might choose to watch a movie, sleep in, or spend time chatting with friends. These are important ways for a young person to decompress after a stressful day. This will help give their minds a break so that they can start fresh when they need to return to work.

Professional counseling can also be helpful for those seeking balance in their lives. Counselors and life coaches may be able to offer advice on sport-life balance and setting healthy boundaries. They may have knowledge of some signs that a person's life may be out of balance, which athletes can use as warning signals to tell them it is time to make changes. If an athlete is feeling very overwhelmed at any point in time, they should speak to someone they trust. That person may be able to help them work through whatever difficulties they are experiencing and figure out what their next steps may be. At the very minimum, athletes who are struggling should talk to their doctor about psychological therapy and review what their options are. Even if they choose not to use them right away, sometimes it can be helpful to know support is available and this way, the athlete will have the information they need if they ever do decide they need professional help.

Saying No

No matter how skilled they are at scheduling or how many planners they use, all people will reach a point where they are full. They simply cannot accommodate any more activities in their lives, even if these activities are things they would like to do. When this happens, the athlete will have to figure out how to decline an invitation to participate or refuse a new commitment. This is one of the most difficult things they will have to learn to do.

It is important that athletes know it's okay to say no to commitments. They should not fear disappointing others because they have to make a difficult choice. A young person's priority should be to look out for themselves, and if committing to a new task would cause them stress, that would be an issue. Plus, limiting the number of things they commit to will mean they are able to dedicate more time to the responsibilities they already have in their lives. It is much better for someone to say no to a commitment right away than it is to start working and realize they do not have the time or energy to follow through on their plans. This will cause them anxiety, and they will have to find someone else to complete the task for them, which is not always an easy process.

When refusing a commitment, it is often best to be as honest as possible. When they are offered a new task, such as being an assistant coach for younger teammates, it is okay to tell the person making the offer that while they are flattered to be considered for the position, their schedule simply will not allow it. They can explain the other commitments they have and that they want to be able to dedicate time to their studies. Most people who work with young athletes understand these demands and will be as accommodating as possible. It is also okay for the athlete to let the person know that if a similar opportunity comes up in the future, when they have more time, they would want to be considered once again. This way, the person will know that the athlete is still interested in the opportunity and may keep them in mind for the future.

Athletes may also encounter situations where they need to prioritize. They might have multiple commitments at the same time and are in a situation where it would be impossible to do everything at once. For example, they might have a training session in the evening and an important paper due the next day. They could ask for an extension on their paper, which some teachers may or may not give. Alternatively, they could aim to work on their assignment after attending practice, which may have them staying up late, and they might not do their best work. Their other option is to skip practice to complete the work, which may mean they miss important drills and their coaches become upset. In any case, there is no perfect scenario.

The athlete may make the difficult decision to skip practice. If they plan their time appropriately and stay ahead of their due dates, this is a situation that will not come up very often. When an athlete constantly finds themselves in a situation where they have to abandon one of their commitments, this might be a sign they have to work harder on planning their schedule. However, every once in a while conflict does happen. In cases like these, when competitive sports aren't an athlete's first priority, the athlete will need to have conversations with their coaches.

The team coordinators might not be pleased the athlete is missing something, particularly if it was important, but talking directly to coaches is a far better option than simply not showing up at all or relaying the message through a teammate. The person should try to give as much notice as they possibly can. If they know a day or two in advance that they will not be present, they should strive to tell their coaches right away. They should also explain the reason for the absence. Many coaches who work with young people are familiar with common conflicts, like school work and family issues, and will be relatively understanding. If they know the athlete has a legitimate reason for not meeting their commitment, they are less likely to be upset. The athlete can even volunteer to make up any missed work on their own time, demonstrating that they are committed to their team and are still willing to put in the extra effort they need to be successful.

If a sports league is not accommodating an athlete who needs to say no to a practice or competition, things can become more challenging. There are cases when a person may need to miss a workout because they need to complete an assignment or they have a family function they cannot miss. In these cases, it can be helpful to involve a parent to help the athlete advocate for themselves. A coach may take the conversation more seriously if an adult is present because they know the athlete is not simply making excuses to avoid practice. If the conversation becomes very difficult, it is okay to ask an adult to take over. It is their job to protect the athlete and look out for their needs, which may include explaining their situation to their sports coach.

In cases when a league consistently makes it difficult to say no when the athlete needs to, they may need to find a new team that is a better fit for them. Some teams are more flexible than others, while some specialize in training young athletes. These organizations may be more accommodating to young people who are trying to balance their sport and their studies. They may have resources in place to offer help when their team members need it, and their practices may be at times that fit around a school schedule. Leaving a league because it is not a good fit does not mean an athlete is done with their sport, and it does not mean they don't love what they do. It only means they are seeking balance, which is a very positive thing overall.

It is critical that an athlete strives to make their sport a part of their lives rather than their entire world. Learning how to balance their competitive sports with their academic and family commitments can be difficult, but it is a skill that all athletes must develop. A sport should complement a person's life rather than consume it completely. For an athlete, part of establishing mental toughness is making space in their world for all the things that make them whole and learning how to say no when they need to.

CONCLUSION

Young athletes have a lot happening in their lives. They are trying to balance an incredible load between their sport, family life, academics, part-time work, and other commitments. These are people who are still growing and finding their way in the world, and they have to do it surrounded by an incredible amount of chaos. Still, many people are happy to commit their time to their sport. They love training and know if they put forward enough effort, they will succeed. This doesn't mean the sport does not come with its own physical and mental challenges.

Just like athletes worry about their physical health, they should also be prioritizing their mental health. People are not "weak" for slowing down, taking a break, or seeking help when they need it. An athlete does not need to "push through" difficult times to prove their worth. They are important and worth looking after. Mental health concerns are legitimate, and the stigma that currently exists about conditions affecting a person's mind often prevents people from seeking the help they need, which is not okay.

When a person is struggling with mental health issues, their physical performance can also be affected. The hormones the body releases during a stress response can have some adverse health effects and impact an athlete's ability to do their best in competitions. Fortunately, there are many ways people are able to reduce the levels of stress hormones in their bodies. By practicing strategies like mindfulness and deep breathing, as well as ensuring they adopt a healthy lifestyle, young people may be able to feel better and perform at a higher level.

Mental health concerns aren't unique to young athletes. Many people in professional sports have also had issues with their mental health, partially due to the demands of their work. Some of them have even come forward to talk about their experiences. By speaking about the things they have been through, these athletes have helped break down some of the stigma that surrounds mental health. They are proof that people can encounter challenges, recover, and still be successful in their sports at the highest level. These people have also shown that when athletes admit that they need help, it is not a sign of weakness.

Athletes can help look after their own mental health and build mental toughness by tapping into the power of their subconscious minds. They can use tools like affirmations to train themselves into adopting a positive mindset. When a person seeks out good things and expects positive outcomes in life, they will feel better and attract more positivity from the world around them. Athletes can train their minds, just like they train their bodies, and make positive thinking a habit they can take with them wherever they go.

They can also work on setting clear goals to give themselves direction. Athletes who know what they are working towards are more likely to remain focused and feel a sense of accomplishment when they finally reach what they have been striving for. There is no one correct way to set goals, but some athletes like to use the SMART framework to help them plan their objectives clearly. When they do achieve their goals, athletes should remember to reward themselves! It is a sign they are making progress, and they deserve to celebrate.

No matter what an athlete is working toward, their mindset is an important contributing factor to their success. People have control over the way they think and the thoughts they choose to listen to. They can choose to focus on constructive thoughts that are going to serve them well rather than negative ones. The more time an athlete spends thinking a thought, the more power it has. People can also make the decision to focus on the things in life they can control, like their own actions and the way they respond to situations, rather than the things they can't. This will help them reclaim power in their lives and reboot the way they think so that they can adopt a positive mindset.

Visualizations can be a useful tool for establishing mental toughness. An athlete can picture an outcome they want and think through an event in vivid detail. This will help them manage their stress levels on competition day and may even improve their performance. Meditation and breath work can also be helpful tools for people looking to manage stress and improve their mental toughness. There are many different strategies a person may use, but all of the ones mentioned in this book have been associated with a reduced stress response and potential health benefits.

An athlete may also want to practice gratitude in their everyday lives. This can be a simple yet effective way for a person to adopt a positive mindset and appreciate everything they already have. They may simply say or write down the things they are thankful for, or they may choose to make their practice more involved and do something like writing a thank-you letter to someone who has done something good. It takes regular repetition to turn something like gratitude into regular practice, but once they do, athletes are likely to enjoy the results they see.

Finally, young people should aim to seek balance in their lives. Their sport is just one part of what they do. Finding balance might mean implementing strategies for planning and making effective use of free time, but it might also mean saying no to certain commitments when they become too much. This can be a difficult thing to do, but athletes owe it to themselves to advocate for what they need.

Using these tools, young athletes can look after their mental health and set themselves up for wellness and success in the future. Many of these are small changes to the way they think, but they can have an incredible impact on the way they live their lives. The tools in this book are just the beginning! With them, young athletes have the ability to shape their futures and achieve incredible success. Their potential is unlimited, and after they have ensured their mental wellness, all they need to worry about is training their way to victory.

ABOUT THE AUTHOR

Thomas Bourne began his career as an accountant and auditor before an extended period as a top-rated emerging market equity research analyst and fund manager. A sports lover and health and wellness fanatic, the unabated pursuit of corporate success and outperformance fueled a relentless curiosity for the workings of the human mind and how we overcome obstacles and achieve our goals. A multitude of personal victories and challenges from his teenage years through to adult life have driven a thirty-year study of the conscious and subconscious mind and our ability as human beings to create the life of our dreams or our own demise. He is the husband of a corporate IT sales executive with an infinite capacity to love and stepfather to two strapping and strong-willed young men making their own mark on the world. When not writing, Thomas spends quality time exploring the outdoors with his dogs, reading, traveling, or enjoying Italian coffee, good wine, and exceptional food. An admitted fanatic of individual and team sports, an ideal weekend will find him engrossed in an international rugby test match or grand slam tennis final.

LEAVE A REVIEW

I would be incredibly thankful if you could write a brief review on Amazon, even if it's just a few sentences!

Just scan the QR code below!

BIBLIOGRAPHY

Arefa Cassoobhoy. (2017, February 6). What Is Cortisol? WebMD; WebMD. https://www.webmd.com/a-to-z-guides/what-is-cortisol

Breathwork Basics, Uses, and Types. (2019, April 29). Healthline. https://www.healthline.com/health/breathwork#exercises

Canfield, J. (2014, April 1). Visualization Techniques to Manifest Desired Outcomes. Jack Canfield. https://jackcanfield.com/blog/visualize-and-affirm-your-desired-outcomes-a-step-by-step-guide/

Cherry, K. (2020, September 1). What is Meditation? Verywell Mind. https://www.verywellmind.com/what-is-meditation-2795927

Christian, L. (2021, November 16). How to Focus on What You Can Control (and Win More Battles). SoulSalt. https://soulsalt.com/focus-on-what-you-can-control/

Cohn, P. (2017, September 14). How to Have Successful Practice Habits | Sports Psychology Articles. Www.peaksports.com. https://www.peaksports.com/sports-psychology-blog/how-to-have-successful-practice-habits-for-athletes/

Davidson, K. (2017). 11 Natural Ways to Lower Your Cortisol Levels. Healthline. https://www.healthline.com/nutrition/ways-to-lower-cortisol

De Lench, B. (n.d.). Nine Ways to Balance Sports and Family Life. Www.momsteam.com. Retrieved July 19, 2022, from https://www.momsteam.com/successful-parenting/survival-skills/balancing-sports-family/nine-ways-to-balance-sports-and-family-

Dopamine vs. serotonin: Similarities, differences, and relationship. (2022, May 11). Www.medicalnewstoday.com. https://www.medicalnewstoday.com/articles/326090#:~:text=Serotonin%20is%20an%20inhibitory%20neurotransmitter

Farrell, D. (n.d.). How Tyson Fury overcame drugs and mental health torment to rule the heavyweight world. Www.sportingnews.com.

Retrieved July 19, 2022, from https://www.sportingnews.com/uk/boxing/news/how-tyson-fury-overcame-drugs-and-mental-health-torment-rule-heavyweight-world/kw9n80zdpgihrwkdmzif8s4v#:~:text=I

How to Use the Power of the Subconscious Mind to Succeed. (2018, April 10). Management 3.0. https://management30.com/blog/subconscious-success/

https://www.briantracy.com/blog/author/brian-tracy. (2018, December 12). The Power of Your Subconscious Mind | Brian Tracy. Brian Tracy's Self Improvement & Professional Development Blog. https://www.briantracy.com/blog/personal-success/understanding-your-subconscious-mind/

mayo clinic. (2019, March 19). Chronic stress puts your health at risk. Mayo Clinic. https://www.mayoclinic.org/healthy-lifestyle/stress-management/in-depth/stress/art-20046037

McDowell, E. (2021, June 6). 12 athletes who've spoken about their mental health struggles. Insider. https://www.insider.com/athletes-mental-health-struggles-depression-2021-6

Mind Tools Content Team. (2009). Personal Goal Setting – Planning to Live Your Life Your Way. Mindtools.com. https://www.mindtools.com/page6.html

Publishing, H. H. (2011, November). Giving thanks can make you happier. Harvard Health. https://www.health.harvard.edu/healthbeat/giving-thanks-can-make-you-happier

Robbins, T. (n.d.). What is Positive Thinking? 5 Ways to Use the Power of Positive Thinking. Tonyrobbins.com. https://www.tonyrobbins.com/positive-thinking/

Robertson, C. (2018, November 29). How Gratitude Can Change Your Life - Dr. Rick Hanson. Dr. Rick Hanson. https://www.rickhanson.net/how-gratitude-can-change-your-life/

Sasson, R. (2020, May 12). Mind Power and the Creative Power of Thoughts. Success Consciousness. https://www.successconsciousness.com/blog/concentration-mind-power/mind-power

Soleimani, S. (2016, January 19). 9 Tips for Balancing School And

Sports. Blog.sisuguard.com. https://blog.sisuguard.com/how-to-find-a-balance-between-school-and-sports

TEDx Talks. (2017). Athletes and Mental Health: The Hidden Opponent | Victoria Garrick | TEDxUSC. In YouTube. https://www.youtube.com/watch?v=Sdk7pLpbIls

The power of affirmations. (n.d.). Www.lifecoach-Directory.org.uk. https://www.lifecoach-directory.org.uk/blog/2020/07/28/the-power-of-affirmations

The Ultimate Goal Setting Process: 7 Steps to Creating Better Goals. (2018, February 6). Www.lucidchart.com. https://www.lucidchart.com/blog/the-ultimate-goal-setting-process-in-7-steps

What Is Visualization Meditation? (2016). Headspace. https://www.headspace.com/meditation/visualization

Wiest, B. (2018, September 12). 13 Ways To Start Training Your Subconscious Mind To Get What You Want. Forbes. https://www.forbes.com/sites/briannawiest/2018/09/12/13-ways-to-start-training-your-subconscious-mind-to-get-what-you-want/

WriterNov 25, C. G., O'Leary, 2019Medically R. S., Psy.D., & P.C. (2019, November 25). 10 Famous Athletes That Struggle With Depression. Www.healthcentral.com. https://www.healthcentral.com/slideshow/famous-athletes-that-struggle-with-depression